I0447893

Milan

Jacques Casanova de Seingalt

[ZHINGOORA BOOKS]

This digital edition is published by Zhingoora Books.

The Cover is Designed by Pallav Sethiya.

Apart from any fair dealing for the purposes of research or private study, or criti-cism or review, this publication may only be reproduced, stored or transmitted, in any form or by any means, with the prior permission in writing of the publishers. All disputes are subject to exclusive jurisdiction of Mandsaur Courts only. For any suggestions and feedback or book on new concept/domain, please contact us at the email given below.

zhingoora_books@yahoo.com

MILAN

CHAPTER XVIII

I Give up Agatha to Lord Percy—I Set out for Milan—The Actress at
Pavia—Countess A * * * B * * *—Disappointment—Marquis Triulzi—Zenobia—The Two Marchionesses Q * * *—The Venetian Barbaro

Far from punishing the Corticelli by making her live with Redegonde, the Count d'Aglie seemed to have encouraged her; and I was not sorry for it, since as long as she did not trouble me any more I did not care how many lovers she had. She had become a great friend of Redegonde's, and did exactly as she pleased, for their duenna was much more easy going than the Pacienza.

Nobody knew of the trick which Lord Percy had played me, and I took care to say nothing about it. However, he did not give up his designs on Agatha, his passion for her was too violent. He hit upon an ingenious method for carrying out his plans. I have already said that Percy was very rich, and spent his money wildly, not caring at what expenditure he gratified his passion. I was the last person to reproach him for his extravagance, and in a country where money is always scarce his guineas opened every door to him.

Four or five days after the ball night, Agatha came to tell me that the manager of the Alexandria Theatre had asked her if she would take the part of second dancer throughout the carnival time.

"He offered me sixty sequins," she added, "and I told him I would let him know by to-morrow. Do you advise me to accept his offer?"

"If you love me, dearest Agatha, you will prove it by refusing all engagements for a year. You know I will let you want for nothing.

"I will get you the best masters, and in that time you can perfect your dancing, and will be able to ask for a first-class appointment, with a salary of five hundred sequins a year."

"Mamma thinks that I should accept the offer, as the dancing on the stage will improve my style, and I can study under a good master all the same. I think myself that dancing in public would do me good."

"There is reason in what you say, but you do not need the sixty sequins. You will dishonour me by accepting such a poor offer, and you will do yourself harm too, as you will not be able to ask for a good salary after taking such a small one."

"But sixty sequins is not so bad for a carnival engagement."

"But you don't want sixty sequins; you can have them without dancing at all. If you love me, I repeat, you will tell the manager that you are going to rest for a year."

"I will do what you please, but it seems to me the best plan would be to ask an exorbitant sum."

"You are right; that is a good idea. Tell him you must be first dancer, and that your salary must be five hundred sequins."

"I will do so, and am only too happy to be able to prove that I love you."

Agatha had plenty of inborn common sense, which only needed development. With that and the beauty which Heaven had given her her future was assured.

She was eventually happy, and she deserved her happiness.

The next day she told me that the manager did not appear at all astonished at her demands.

"He reflected a few minutes," said she, "and told me he must think it over, and would see me again. It would be amusing if he took me at my word, would it not?"

"Yes, but we should then have to enquire whether he is a madman or a beggar on the verge of bankruptcy."

"And if he turns out to be a man of means?"

"In that case you would be obliged to accept."

"That is easily said and easily done, but have I sufficient talent? Where shall I find an actor to dance with me?"

"I will engage to find you one. As to talent, you have enough and to spare; but you will see that it will come to nothing."

All the time I felt a presentiment that she would be engaged, and I was right. The manager came to her the next day, and offered her the agreement for her signature. She was quite alarmed, and sent for me. I called at her house, and finding the manager there asked him what security he could give for the fulfilment of his part of the engagement.

He answered by naming M. Martin, a banker of my acquaintance, who would be his surety. I could make no objection to this, and the agreement was made out in duplicate in good form.

On leaving Agatha I went to M. Raiberti and told him the story. He shared my astonishment that M. Martin should become surety for the manager whom he knew, and whose financial position was by no means good; but the next day the problem was solved, for in spite of the secrecy that had been observed we found out that it was Lord Percy who was behind the manager. I might still bar the Englishman's way by continuing to keep Agatha, in spite of his five hundred sequins, but I was obliged to return to France after Easter to wait on Madame d'Urfe, and afterwards, peace having been concluded, I thought it would be a good opportunity for seeing England. I therefore determined to abandon Agatha, taking care to bind her new lover to provide for her, and I proceeded to make a friend of the nobleman.

I was curious to see how he would win Agatha's good graces, for she did not love him, and physically he was not attractive.

In less than a week we had become intimate. We supped together every night either at his house or mine, and Agatha and her mother were always of the party. I concluded that his attentions would soon touch Agatha's heart, and that finding herself so beloved she would end by loving. This was enough to make me determine not to put any obstacles in their way, and I resolved to leave Turin earlier than I had intended. In consequence I spoke as follows to Lord Percy, while we were breakfasting together:

"My lord, you know that I love Agatha, and that she loves me, nevertheless I am your friend, and since you adore her I will do my best to hasten your bliss. I will leave you in possession of this treasure, but you must promise that when you abandon her you will give her two thousand guineas."

"My dear sir," said he, "I will give them her now if you like."

"No, my lord, I do not wish her to know anything about our agreement while you are living happily together."

"Then I will give you a bond binding myself to pay her the two thousand guineas when we separate."

"I don't want that, the word of an Englishman is enough; but since we cannot command the fates, and may die without having time to put our affairs in order, I wish you to take such steps as may seem convenient to you, whereby that sum would go to her after your death."

"I give you my word on it."

"That is enough; but I have one other condition to make."

"Say on."

"It is that you promise to say nothing to Agatha before my departure."

"I swear I will not."

"Very good; and on my part I promise to prepare her for the change:"

The same day the Englishman, whose love grew hotter and hotter, made
Agatha and her mother rich presents, which under any other circumstances
I should not have allowed them to accept.

I lost no time in preparing Agatha and her mother for the impending change. They seemed affected, but I knew they would soon get reconciled to the situation. Far from giving me any cause for complaint, Agatha was more affectionate than ever. She listened attentively to my advice as to her conduct towards her new lover and the world in general, and promised to follow it. It was to this advice that she owed her happiness, for Percy made her fortune. However, she did not leave the theatre for some years, when we shall hear more of her.

I was not the man to take presents from my equals, and Percy no doubt being aware of that succeeded in making me a handsome present in a very singular way. I told him that I thought of paying a visit to England and requested him to give me a letter of introduction to the duchess, his mother, whereon he drew out a portrait of her set with magnificent diamonds, and gave it to me, saying,—

"This is the best letter I can give you. I will write and tell her that you will call and give her the portrait, unless, indeed, she likes to leave it in your hands."

"I hope my lady will think me worthy of such an honour."

There are certain ideas, it seems to me, which enter no head but an Englishman's.

I was invited by Count A—— B—— to Milan, and the countess wrote me a charming letter, begging me to get her two pieces of sarcenet, of which she enclosed the patterns.

After taking leave of all my friends and acquaintances I got a letter of credit on the banker, Greppi, and started for the capital of Lombardy.

My separation from Agatha cost me many tears, but not so many as those shed by her. Her mother wept also, for she loved me, and was grateful for all my kindness to her daughter. She said again and again that she could never have borne any rival but her own daughter, while the latter sobbed out that she wished she had not to part from me.

I did not like Passano, so I sent him to his family at Genoa, giving him the wherewithal to live till I came for him. As to my man, I dismissed him for good reasons and took another, as I was obliged to have somebody; but since I lost my Spaniard I have never felt confidence in any of my servants.

I travelled with a Chevalier de Rossignan, whose acquaintance I had made, and we went by Casal to see the opera-bouffe there.

Rossignan was a fine man, a good soldier, fond of wine and women, and, though he was not learned, he knew the whole of Dante's Divine Comedy by heart. This was his hobby-horse, and he was always quoting it, making the passage square with his momentary feelings. This made him insufferable in society, but he was an amusing companion for anyone who knew the sublime poet, and could appreciate his numerous and rare beauties. Nevertheless he made me privately give in my assent to the proverb, Beware of the man of one book. Otherwise he was intelligent, statesmanlike, and good-natured. He made himself known at Berlin by his services as ambassador to the King of Sardinia.

There was nothing interesting in the opera at Casal, so I went to Pavia, where, though utterly unknown, I was immediately welcomed by the Marchioness Corti, who received all strangers of any importance. In 1786 I made the acquaintance of her son, an admirable man, who honoured me with his friendship, and died quite young in Flanders with the rank of major-general. I wept bitterly for his loss, but tears, after all, are but an idle tribute to those who cause them to flow. His good qualities had endeared him to all his acquaintances, and if he had lived longer he would undoubtedly have risen to high command in the army.

I only stopped two days at Pavia, but it was decreed that I should get myself talked of, even in that short time.

At the second ballet at the opera an actress dressed in a tippet held out her cap to the bones as if to beg an alms, while she was dancing a pas de deux. I was in the Marchioness of Corti's box, and when the girl held out her cap to me I was moved by feelings of ostentation and benevolence to draw forth my purse and drop it in. It contained about twenty ducats. The girl took it, thanked me with a smile, and the pit applauded loudly. I asked the Marquis Belcredi, who was near me, if she had a lover.

"She has a penniless French officer, I believe," he replied; "there he is, in the pit."

I went back to my inn, and was supping with M. Basili, a Modenese colonel, when the ballet girl, her mother, and her younger sister came to thank me for my providential gift. "We are so poor," said the girl.

I had almost done supper, and I asked them all to sup with me after the performance the next day. This offer was quite a disinterested one, and it was accepted.

I was delighted to have made a woman happy at so little expense and without any ulterior objects, and I was giving orders to the landlord for the supper, when Clairmont, my man, told me that a French officer wanted to speak to me. I had him in, and asked what I could do for him.

"There are three courses before you, Mr. Venetian," said he, "and you can take which you like. Either countermand this supper, invite me to come to it, or come and measure swords with me now."

Clairmont, who was attending to the fire, did not give me time to reply, but seized a burning brand and rushed on the officer, who thought it best to escape. Luckily for him the door of my room was open. He made such a noise in running downstairs that the waiter came out and caught hold of him, thinking he had stolen something; but Clairmont, who was pursuing him with his firebrand, had him released.

This adventure became town talk directly. My servant, proud of his exploit and sure of my approval, came to tell me that I need not be afraid of going out, as the officer was only a braggart. He did not even draw his sword on the waiter who had caught hold of him, though the man only had a knife in his belt.

"At all events," he added, "I will go out with you."

I told him that he had done well this time, but that for the future he must not interfere in my affairs.

"Sir," he replied, "your affairs of this kind are mine too, I shall take care not to go beyond my duty."

With this speech, which I thought very sensible, though I did not tell him so, he took one of my pistols and saw to the priming, smiling at me significantly.

All good French servants are of the same stamp as Clairmont; they are devoted and intelligent, but they all think themselves cleverer than their masters, which indeed is often the case, and when they are sure of it they become the masters of their masters, tyrannize over them, and give them marks of contempt which the foolish gentlemen endeavour to conceal. But when the master knows how to make himself respected, the Clairmonts are excellent.

The landlord of my inn sent a report of the affair to the police, and the
French officer was banished from the town the same day. At dinner Colonel
Basili asked to hear the story, and said that no one but a French officer
would think of attacking a man in his own room in such a foolish manner.
I differed from him.

"The French are brave," I replied, "but generally they are perfectly polite and have wonderful tact. Wretchedness and love, joined to a false spirit of courage, makes a fool of a man all the world over."

At supper the ballet-girl thanked me for ridding her of the poor devil, who (as she said) was always threatening to kill her, and wearied her besides. Though she was not beautiful, there was something captivating about this girl. She was graceful, well-mannered, and intelligent, her mouth was well-shaped, and her eyes large and expressive. I think I should have found her a good bargain, but as I wanted to get away from Pavia, and piqued myself on having been good-natured without ulterior motive, I bade her farewell after supper, with many thanks for her kindness in coming. My politeness seemed rather to confuse her, but she went away reiterating her gratitude.

Next day I dined at the celebrated Chartreuse, and in the evening I reached Milan, and got out at Count A—— B——'s, who had not expected me till the following day.

The countess, of whom my fancy had made a perfect woman, disappointed me dreadfully. It is always so when passion gives reins to the imagination. The Countess was certainly pretty, though too small, and I might still have loved her, in spite of my disappointment, but at our meeting she greeted me with a gravity that was not to my taste, and which gave me a dislike to her.

After the usual compliments, I gave her the two pieces of sarcenet she had commissioned me to get. She thanked me, telling me that her confessor would reimburse me for my expenditure. The count then took me to my room, and left me there till supper. It was nicely furnished, but I felt ill at ease, and resolved to leave in a day or two if the countess remained immovable. Twenty-four hours was as much as I cared to give her.

We made a party of four at supper; the count talking all the time to draw me out, and to hide his wife's sulkiness. I answered in the same gay strain, speaking to his wife, however, in the hope of rousing her. It was all lost labour. The little woman only replied by faint smiles which vanished almost as they came, and by monosyllabic answers of the briefest description, without taking her eyes off the dishes which she thought tasteless; and it was to the priest, who was the fourth person present, that she addressed her complaints, almost speaking affably to him.

Although I liked the count very well, I could not help pronouncing his wife decidedly ungracious. I was looking at her to see if I could find any justification for her ill humour on her features, but as soon as she saw me she turned away in a very marked manner, and began to speak about nothing to the priest. This conduct offended me, and I laughed heartily at her contempt, or her designs on me, for as she had not fascinated me at all I was safe from her tyranny.

After supper the sarcenet was brought in; it was to be used for a dress with hoops, made after the extravagant fashion then prevailing.

The count was grieved to see her fall so short of the praises he had lavished on her, and came to my room with me, begging me to forgive her Spanish ways, and saying that she would be very pleasant when she knew me better.

The count was poor, his house was small, his furniture shabby, and his footman's livery threadbare; instead of plate he had china, and one of the countess's maids was chief cook. He had no carriages nor horses, not even a saddle horse of any kind. Clairmont gave me all this information, and added that he had to sleep in a little kitchen, and was to share his bed with the man who had waited at table.

I had only one room, and having three heavy trunks found myself very uncomfortable, and I decided on seeking some other lodging more agreeable to my tastes.

The count came early in the morning to ask what I usually took for breakfast.

"My dear count," I replied, "I have enough fine Turin chocolate to go all round. Does the countess like it?"

"Very much, but she won't take it unless it is made by her woman."

"Here are six pounds: make her accept it, and tell her that if I hear anything about payment I shall take it back."

"I am sure she will accept it, and thank you too. Shall I have your carriage housed?"

"I shall be extremely obliged to you, and I shall be glad if you would get me a hired carriage, and a guide for whom you can answer."

"It shall be done."

The count was going out when the priest, who had supped with us the night before, came in to make his bow. He was a man of forty-one of the tribe of domestic chaplains who are so common in Italy—who, in return for keeping the accounts of the house, live with its master and mistress. In the morning this priest said mass in a neighbouring church, for the rest of the day he either occupied himself with the cares of the house, or was the lady's obedient servant.

As soon as we were alone he begged me to say that he had paid me the three hundred Milanese crowns for the sarcenet, if the countess asked me about it.

"Dear, dear, abbe!" said I, laughing, "this sort of thing is not exactly proper in a man of your sacred profession. How can you advise me to tell a lie? No, sir; if the countess asks me any such impertinent question, I shall tell her the truth."

"I am sure she will ask you, and if you answer like that I shall suffer for it."

"Well, sir, if you are in the wrong you deserve to suffer."

"But as it happens, I should be blamed for nothing."

"Well, go and tell her it's a present; and if she won't have that, tell her I am in no hurry to be paid."

"I see, sir, that you don't know the lady or the way in which this house is managed. I will speak to her husband."

In a quarter of an hour the count told me that he owed me a lot of money, which he hoped to pay back in the course of Lent, and that I must add the sarcenet to the account. I embraced him and said that he would have to keep the account himself, as I never noted down any of the moneys that I was only too happy to lend to my friends.

"If your wife asks me whether I have received the money, be sure I will answer in the affirmative."

He went out shedding grateful tears, while I felt indebted to him for having given me the opportunity of doing him a service; for I was very fond of him.

In the morning, the countess being invisible, I watched my man spreading out my suits over the chairs, amongst them being some handsome women's cloaks, and a rich red dress deeply trimmed with fur, which had been originally intended for the luckless Corticelli. I should no doubt have given it to Agatha, if I had continued to live with her, and I should have made a mistake, as such a dress was only fit for a lady of rank.

At one o'clock I received another visit from the count, who told me that the countess was going to introduce me to their best friend. This was the Marquis Triuizi, a man of about, my own age, tall, well made, squinting slightly, and with all the manner of a nobleman. He told me that besides coming to have the honour of my acquaintance, he also came to enjoy the fire, "for," said he, "there's only one fireplace in the house and that's in your room."

As all the chairs were covered, the marquis drew the countess on to his knee and made her sit there like a baby; but she blushed, and escaped from his grasp. The marquis laughed heartily at her confusion, and she said,—

"Is it possible that a man of your years has not yet learnt to respect a woman?"

"Really, countess," said he, "I thought it would be very disrespectful to continue sitting while you were standing."

While Clairmont was taking the clothes off the chairs, the marquis noticed the mantles and the beautiful dress, and asked me if I were expecting a lady.

"No," said I, "but I hope to find someone at Milan who will be worthy of such presents." I added, "I know the Prince Triulzi, at Venice; I suppose he is of your family?"

"He says he is, and it may be so; but I am certainly not a member of his family."

This let me know that I should do well to say no more about the prince.

"You must stay to dinner, marquis," said Count A—— B——; "and as you only like dishes prepared by your own cook you had better send for them."

The marquis agreed, and we made good cheer. The table was covered with fair linen and handsome plate, the wine was good and plentiful, and the servants quick and well dressed. I could now understand the marquis's position in the house. It was his wit and mirth which kept the conversation going, and the countess came in for a share of his pleasantries, while she scolded him for his familiarity.

I could see, however, that the marquis did not want to humiliate her; on the contrary, he was fond of her, and only wished to bring down her exaggerated pride. When he saw her on the point of bursting into tears of rage and shame, he quieted her down by saying that no one in Milan respected her charms and her high birth more than he.

After dinner the tailor who was to measure the countess for a domino for the ball was announced. On the marquis's praising the colours and the beauty of the materials, she told him that I had brought her the sarcenet from Turin, and this reminded her to ask me whether I had been paid.

"Your husband settled with me," said I, "but you have given me a lesson I can never forget."

"What lesson?" said the marquis.

"I had hoped that the countess would have deigned to receive this poor present at my hands."

"And she wouldn't take it? It's absurd, on my life."

"There is nothing to laugh at," said the countess, "but you laugh at everything."

While the man was measuring her, she complained of feeling cold, as she was in her stays, and her beautiful breast was exposed. Thereupon, the marquis put his hands on it, as if he were quite accustomed to use such familiarities. But the Spaniard, no doubt ashamed because of my presence, got into a rage, and abused him in the most awful manner, while he laughed pleasantly, as if he could calm the storm when he pleased. This was enough to inform me of the position in which they stood to one another, and of the part I ought to take.

We remained together till the evening, when the countess and the marquis went to the opera, and the count came with me to my room, till my carriage was ready to take us there too. The opera had begun when we got in, and the first person I noticed on the stage was my dear Therese Palesi, whom I had left at Florence. It was a pleasant surprise to me, and I foresaw that we should renew our sweet interviews while I remained at Milan I was discreet enough to say nothing to the count about his wife's charms, or the way their house was managed. I saw that the place was taken, and the odd humours of the lady prevented my falling in love with her. After the second act we went to the assembly rooms, where five or six banks at faro were being held; I staked and lost a hundred ducats as if to pay for my welcome, and then rose from the table.

At supper the countess seemed to unbend a little, she condoled with me on my loss, and I said that I was glad of it as it made her speak so.

Just as I rang my bell the next morning, Clairmont told me that a woman wanted to speak to me.

"Is she young?"

"Both young and pretty, sir."

"That will do nicely, shew her in."

I saw a simply dressed girl, who reminded me of Leah. She was tall and beautiful, but had not as high pretensions as the Jewess; as she only wanted to know whether she could do my washing for me. I was quite taken with her. Clairmont had just brought me my chocolate, and I asked her to sit down on the bed; but she answered modestly that she did not want to trouble me, and would come again when I was up.

"Do you live at any distance?"

"I live on the ground floor of this house."

"All by yourself?"

"No sir, I have my father and mother."

"And what is your name?"

"Zenobia."

"Your name is as pretty as you are. Will you give me your hand to kiss?"

"I can't," she replied, with a smile, "my hand is another's."

"You are engaged, are you?"

"Yes, to a tailor, and we are going to be married before the end of the carnival."

"Is he rich or handsome?"

"Neither the one nor the other."

"Then why are you going to marry him?"

"Because I want to have a house of my own."

"I like you, and will stand your friend. Go and fetch your tailor. I will give him some work to do."

As soon as she went out I got up and told Clairmont to put my linen on a table. I had scarcely finished dressing when she came back with her tailor. It was a striking contrast, for he was a little shrivelled-up man, whose appearance made one laugh.

"Well, master tailor," said I, "so you are going to marry this charming girl?"

"Yes, sir, the banns have been published already."

"You are a lucky fellow indeed to have so much happiness in store. When are you going to marry her?"

"In ten or twelve days."

"Why not to-morrow?"

"Your worship is in a great hurry."

"I think I should be, indeed," said I, laughing, "if I were in your place. I want you to make me a domino for the ball to-morrow."

"Certainly, sir; but your excellency must find me the stuff, for nobody in Milan would give me credit for it, and I couldn't afford to lay out so much money in advance."

"When you are married you will have money and credit too. In the meanwhile here are ten sequins for you."

He went away in high glee at such a windfall.

I gave Zenobia some lace to do up, and asked her if she was afraid of having a jealous husband.

"He is neither jealous nor amorous," she replied. "He is only marrying me because I earn more than he does."

"With your charms I should have thought you might have made a better match."

"I have waited long enough; I have got tired of maidenhood. Besides, he is sharp if he is not handsome, and perhaps a keen head is better than a handsome face."

"You are sharp enough yourself, anyhow. But why does he put off the wedding?"

"Because he hasn't got any money, and wants to have a fine wedding for his relations to come to. I should like it myself."

"I think you are right; but I can't see why you should not let an honest man kiss your hand."

"That was only a piece of slyness to let you know I was to be married. I have no silly prejudices myself."

"Ah, that's better! Tell your future husband that if he likes me to be the patron of the wedding I will pay for everything."

"Really?"

"Yes, really. I will give him twenty-five sequins on the condition that he spends it all on the wedding."

"Twenty-five sequins! That will make people talk; but what care we? I will give you an answer to-morrow."

"And a kiss now?"

"With all my heart."

Zenobia went away in great delight, and I went out to call on my banker and dear Therese.

When the door was opened the pretty maid recognized me, and taking me by the hand led me to her mistress, who was just going to get up. Her emotion at seeing me was so great that she could not utter a word, but only claps me to her breast.

Our natural transports over, Therese told me that she had got tired of her husband, and that for the last six months they had not been living together. She had made him an allowance to get rid of him, and he lived on it at Rome.

"And where is Cesarino?"

"In this town. You can see him whenever you like."

"Are you happy?"

"Quite. People say that I have a lover, but it is not true; and you can see me at any time with perfect liberty."

We spent two pleasant hours in telling each other of our experiences since our last meeting, and then, finding her as fresh and fair as in the season of our early loves, I asked her if she had vowed to be faithful to her husband.

"At Florence," she replied, "I was still in love with him; but now, if I am still pleasing in your eyes, we can renew our connection, and live together till we die."

"I will soon shew you, darling, that I love you as well as ever."

She answered only by giving herself up to my embrace.

After action and contemplation I left her as amorous as she had been eighteen years before, but my passion found too many new objects to remain constant long.

Countess A—— B—— began to be more polite. "I know where you have been," said she, with a pleased air; "but if you love that person, you will not go and see her again, or else her lover will leave her."

"Then I would take his place, madam."

"You are right in amusing yourself with women who know how to earn your presents. I am aware that you never give anything till you have received evident proofs of their affection."

"That has always been my principle."

"It's an excellent way to avoid being duped. The lover of the person you have been with kept a lady in society for some time in great splendour, but all the rest of us despised her."

"Why so, if you please?"

"Because she lowered herself so terribly. Greppi is absolutely a man of no family whatever."

Without expressing my surprise at the name of Greppi, I replied that a man need not be well born to be an excellent lover.

"The only thing needful," said I, "is a fine physique and plenty of money, and those ladies who despised their friend were either ridiculously proud or abominably envious. I have not the slightest doubt that if they could find any more Gieppis they would be willing enough to lower themselves."

She would doubtless have made a sharp reply, for what I had said had angered her; but the Marquis Triulzi arriving, she went out with him, while her husband and myself went to a place where there was a bank at faro, the banker only having a hundred sequins before him.

I took a card and staked small sums like the rest of the company. After losing twenty ducats I left the place.

As we were going to the opera the poor count told me I had made him lose ten ducats on his word of honour, and that he did not know how he could pay it by the next day. I pitied him, and gave him the money without a word; for misery has always appealed strongly to me. Afterwards I lost two hundred ducats at the same bank to which I had lost money the evening before. The count was in the greatest distress. He did not know that Greppi, whom his proud wife considered so worthless, had a hundred thousand francs of my money, and that I possessed jewellery to an even greater amount.

The countess, who had seen me lose, asked me if I would sell my beautiful dress.

"They say it's worth a thousand sequins," said she.

"Yes, that is so; but I would sell everything I possess before parting with any of the articles which I intend for the fair sex."

"Marquis Triulzi wants it badly to present to someone."

"I am very sorry, but I cannot sell it to him."

She went away without a word, but I could see that she was exceedingly vexed at my refusal.

As I was leaving the opera-house I saw Therese getting into her sedan-chair. I went up to her, and told her that I was sure she was going to sup with her lover. She whispered in my ear that she was going to sup by herself, and that I might come if I dared. I gave her an agreeable surprise by accepting the invitation.

"I will expect you, then," she said.

I asked the count to ride home in my carriage, and taking a chair I reached Therese's house just as she was going in.

What a happy evening we had! We laughed heartily when we told each other our thoughts.

"I know you were in love with Countess A—— B——," said she, "and I felt sure you would not dare to come to supper with me."

"And I thought I should confound you by accepting your invitation, as I knew Greppi was your lover."

"He is my friend," she replied. "If he loves me in any other way than that of friendship, I pity him, for as yet he has not discovered the secret of seduction."

"Do you think he ever will?"

"No, I don't. I am rich."

"Yes, but he is richer than you."

"I know that, but I think he loves his money better than he loves me."

"I understand. You will make him happy if he loves you well enough to ruin himself."

"That is it, but it will never come to pass. But here we are, together again after a divorce of nearly twenty years. I don't think you will find any change in me."

"That is a privilege which nature grants to the fair sex only. You will find me changed, but you will be able to work miracles."

This was a piece of politeness, for she was hardly capable of working any miracle. However, after an excellent supper, we spent two hours in amorous raptures, and then Morpheus claimed us for his own. When we awoke I did not leave her before giving her a good day equal to the good night which had sent us to sleep.

When I got back I found the fair Zenobia, who said the tailor was ready to marry her next Sunday if my offer was not a joke.

"To convince you of the contrary," said I, "here are the twenty-five sequins."

Full of gratitude she let herself fall into my arms, and I covered her mouth and her beautiful bosom with my fiery kisses. Therese had exhausted me, so I did not go any further, but the girl no doubt attributed my self-restraint to the fact that the door was open. I dressed carefully, and made myself look less weary, and to freshen myself up I had a long drive in an open carriage.

When I returned, I found the Marquis of Triulzi teasing the countess as usual. On that day he furnished the dinner, and it was consequently, a very good one.

The conversation turned on the dress in my possession, and the countess told the marquis, like an idiot, that it was destined for the lady who would make me desirous and gratify my desire.

With exquisite politeness the marquis told me that I deserved to enjoy favours at a cheaper rate.

"I suppose you will be giving it to the person with whom you spent the night," said the countess.

"That's an impossibility," I answered, "for I spent the night in play."

Just then Clairmont came in, and told me an officer wanted to speak to me. I went to the door, and saw a handsome young fellow, who greeted me with an embrace. I recognized him as Barbaro, the son of a Venetian noble, and brother of the fair and famous Madame Gritti Scombro, of whom I spoke ten years ago, whose husband had died in the citadel of Cattaro, where the State Inquisitors had imprisoned him. My young friend had also fallen into disgrace with the despotic Inquisitors. We had been good friends during the year before my imprisonment, but I had heard nothing of him since.

Barbaro told me the chief incidents in a life that had been adventurous enough, and informed me that he was now in the service of the Duke of Modena, the Governor of Milan.

"I saw you losing money at Canano's bank," said he, "and remembering our old friendship I want to communicate to you a sure way of winning money. All that is necessary is for me to introduce you to a club of young men who are very fond of play, and cannot possibly win."

"Where does this club meet?"

"In an extremely respectable house. If you agree I will keep the bank myself, and I am sure of winning. I want you to lend me capital, and I only ask a fourth of the profits."

"I suppose you can hold the cards well."

"You are right."

This was as much as to tell me that he was an adroit sharper, or, in other words, a skilful corrector of fortune's mistakes. He concluded by saying that I should find something worth looking at in the house he had mentioned.

"My dear sir," I replied, "I will give you my decision after seeing the club to which you want to introduce me."

"Will you be at the theatre coffee-house at three o'clock to-morrow?"

"Yes, but I hope to see you at the ball in the evening."

Zenobia's betrothed brought me my domino, and the countess had hers already. As the ball did not begin till the opera was over, I went to hear Therese's singing. In the interval between the acts I lost another two hundred sequins, and then went home to dress for the ball. The countess said that if I would be kind enough to take her to the ball in my carriage and fetch her home in it, she would not send for the Marquis Triulzi's. I replied that I was at her service.

Under the impression that the fair Spaniard had only given me the preference to enable me to take liberties with her, I told her I should be very glad to give her the dress, and that the only condition was that I should spent a night with her.

"You insult me cruelly," said she, "you must know my character better than that."

"I know everything, my dear countess; but, after all, the insult's nothing; you can easily forgive me if you pluck up a little spirit; trample on a foolish prejudice; get the dress, and make me happy for a whole night long."

"That it all very well when one is in love, but you must confess that your coarse way of speaking is more likely to make me hate you than love you."

"I use that style, because I want to come to the point; I have no time to waste. And you, countess, must confess in your turn, that you would be delighted to have me sighing at your feet."

"It would be all the same to me, I don't think I could love you."

"Then we are agreed on one point at all events, for I love you no more than you love me."

"And yet you would spend a thousand sequins for the pleasure of passing a night with me."

"Not at all, I don't want to sleep with you for the sake of the pleasure, but to mortify your infernal pride, which becomes you so ill."

God knows what the fierce Spaniard would have answered, but at that moment the carriage stopped at the door of the theatre. We parted, and after I had got tired of threading my way amidst the crowd I paid a visit to the gaming-room, hoping to regain the money I had lost. I had more than five hundred sequins about me and a good credit at the bank, but I certainly did my best to lose everything I had. I sat down at Canano's bank, and noticing that the poor count, who followed me wherever I went, was the only person who knew me, I thought I should have a lucky evening. I only punted on one card, and spent four hours without losing or gaining. Towards the end, wishing to force fortune's favour, I lost rapidly, and left all my money in the hands of the banker. I went back to the ball-room, where the countess rejoined me, and we returned home.

When we were in the carriage, she said,—

"You lost an immense sum, and I am very glad of it. The marquis will give you a thousand sequins, and the money will bring you luck."

"And you, too, for I suppose you will have the dress?"

"Maybe."

"No, madam, you shall never have it in this way, and you know the other.
I despise a thousand sequins."

"And I despise you and your presents."

"You may despise me as much as you please, and you may be sure I despise you."

With these polite expressions we reached the house. When I got to my room I found the count there with a long face, as if he wanted to pity me but dared not do it. However, my good temper gave him the courage to say:—

"Triulzi will give you a thousand sequins; that will fit you up again."

"For the dress you mean?"

"Yes."

"I wanted to give it to your wife, but she said she would despise it, coming from my hands."

"You astonish me; she is mad after it. You must have wounded her haughty temper in some way or another. But sell it, and get the thousand sequins."

"I will let you know to-morrow."

I slept four or five hours, and then rose and went out in my great coat to call on Greppi, for I had no more money. I took a thousand sequins, begging him not to tell my affairs to anyone. He replied that my affairs were his own, and that I could count on his secrecy. He complimented me on the esteem in which Madame Palesi held me, and said he hoped to meet me at supper at her house one night.

"Such a meeting would give me the greatest pleasure," I replied.

On leaving him I called on Therese, but as there were some people with her I did not stay long. I was glad to see that she knew nothing about my losses or my affairs. She said that Greppi wanted to sup with me at her house, and that she would let me know when the day was fixed. When I got home I found the count in front of my fire.

"My wife is in a furious rage with you," said he, "and won't tell me why."

"The reason is, my dear count, that I won't let her accept the dress from any hand but mine. She told me that she should despise it as a gift from me, but she has nothing to be furious about that I know."

"It's some mad notion of hers, and I don't know what to make of it. But pray attend to what I am about to say to you. You despise a thousand sequins—good. I congratulate you. But if you are in a position to despise a sum which would make me happy, offer up a foolish vanity on the shrine of friendship, take the thousand sequins, and lend them to me, and let my wife have the dress, for of course he will give it her."

This proposal made me roar with laughter, and certainly it was of a nature to excite the hilarity of a sufferer from confirmed melancholia, which I was far from being. However, I stopped laughing when I saw how the poor count blushed from shame. I kissed him affectionately to calm him, but at last I was cruel enough to say,

"I will willingly assist you in this arrangement. I will sell the dress to the marquis as soon as you please, but I won't lend you the money. I'll give it to you in the person of your wife at a private interview; but when she receives me she must not only be polite and complaisant, but as gentle as a lamb. Go and see if it can be arranged, my dear count; 'tis absolutely my last word."

"I will see," said the poor husband; and with that he went out.

Barbaro kept his appointment with exactitude. I made him get into my carriage, and we alighted at a house at the end of Milan. We went to the first floor, and there I was introduced to a fine-looking old man, an amiable lady of pleasing appearance, and then to two charming cousins. He introduced me as a Venetian gentleman in disgrace with the State Inquisitors, like himself, adding, that as I was a rich bachelor their good or ill favour made no difference to me.

He said I was rich, and I looked like it. My luxury of attire was dazzling: My rings, my snuff-boxes, my chains, my diamonds, my jewelled cross hanging on my breast-all gave me the air of an important personage. The cross belonged to the Order of the Spur the Pope had given me, but as I had carefully taken the spur away

---

it was not known to what order I belonged. Those who might be curious did not dare to ask me, for one can no more enquire of a knight what order he belongs to, than one can say to a lady how old are you? I wore it till 1785, when the Prince Palatine of Russia told me in private that I would do well to get rid of the thing.

"It only serves to dazzle fools," said he, "and here you have none such to deal with."

I followed his advice, for he was a man of profound intelligence. Nevertheless, he removed the corner-stone of the kingdom of Poland. He ruined it by the same means by which he had made it greater.

The old man to whom Barbaro presented me was a marquis. He told me that he knew Venice, and as I was not a patrician I could live as pleasantly anywhere else. He told me to consider his house and all he possessed as mine.

The two young marchionesses had enchanted me; they were almost ideal beauties. I longed to enquire about them of some good authority, for I did not put much faith in Barbaro.

In half an hour the visitors commenced to come on foot and in carriages. Among the arrivals were several pretty and well-dressed girls, and numerous smart young men all vying with each other in their eagerness to pay court to the two cousins. There were twenty of us in all. We sat round a large table, and began to play a game called bankruptcy. After amusing myself for a couple of hours in losing sequins, I went out with Barbaro to the opera.

"The two young ladies are two incarnate angels," I said to my countryman. "I shall pay my duty to them, and shall find out in a few days whether they are for me. As for the gaming speculation, I will lend you two hundred sequins; but I don't want to lose the money, so you must give me good security."

"To that I agree willingly, but I am certain of giving it you back with good interest."

"You shall have a half share and not twenty-five per cent., and I must strongly insist that nobody shall know of my having anything to do with your bank. If I hear any rumours, I shall bet heavily on my own account."

"You may be sure I shall keep the secret; it is to my own interest to have it believed that I am my own capitalist."

"Very good. Come to me early to-morrow morning, and bring me good security, and you shall have the money."

He embraced me in the joy of his heart.

The picture of the two fair ladies was still in my brain, and I was thinking of enquiring of Greppi when I chanced to see Triulzi in the pit of the opera-house. He saw me at the same moment, and came up to me, saying gaily that he was sure I had had a bad dinner, and that I had much better dine with him every day.

"You make me blush, marquis, for not having called on you yet."

"No, no; there can be nothing of that kind between men of the world, who know the world's worth."

"We are agreed there, at all events."

"By the way, I hear you have decided on selling me that handsome dress of yours. I am really very much obliged to you, and will give you the fifteen thousand livres whenever you like."

"You can come and take it to-morrow morning."

He then proceeded to tell me about the various ladies I noticed in the theatre. Seizing the opportunity, I said,—

"When I was in church the other day I saw two exquisite beauties. A man at my side told me they were cousins, the Marchionesses Q—— and I——, I think he said. Do you know them? I am quite curious to hear about them."

"I know them. As you say, they are charming. It's not very difficult to obtain access to them; and I suppose they are good girls, as I have not heard their names in connection with any scandal. However, I know that Mdlle. F has a lover, but it is a great secret; he is the only son of one of the noblest of our families. Unfortunately, they are not rich; but if they are clever, as I am sure they are, they may make good matches. If you like I can get someone to introduce you there."

"I haven't made up my mind yet. I may be able to forget them easily only having seen them once. Nevertheless, I am infinitely obliged to you for your kind offer."

After the ballet I went into the assembly-room and I heard "there he is" several times repeated as I came in. The banker made me a bow, and offered me a place next to him. I sat down and he handed me a pack of cards. I punted, and with such inveterate bad luck that in less than an hour I lost seven hundred sequins. I should probably have lost all the money I had in my pocket if Canano had not been obliged to go away. He gave the cards to a man whose looks displeased me, and I rose and went home and got into bed directly, so as not to be obliged to conceal my ill temper.

In the morning Barbaro came to claim the two hundred sequins. He gave me the right to sequestrate his pay by way of surety. I do not think I should have had the heart to exercise my rights if things had gone wrong, but I liked to have some control over him. When I went out I called on Greppi, and took two thousand sequins in gold.

CHAPTER XIX

*Humiliation of The Countess—Zenobia's Wedding—Faro
Conquest of The Fair
Irene—Plan for a Masquerade*

On my return I found the count with one of the marquis's
servants, who gave me a note, begging me to send the dress, which
I did directly.

"The marquis will dine with us," said the count, "and, no doubt, he
will bring the money with him for this treasure."

"You think it a treasure, then?"

"Yes, fit for a queen to wear."

"I wish the treasure had the virtue of giving you a crown; one head-
dress is as good as another."

The poor devil understood the allusion, and as I liked him I
reproached myself for having humiliated him unintentionally,
but I could not resist the temptation to jest. I hastened to smooth
his brow by saying that as soon as I got the money for the dress I
would take it to the countess.

"I have spoken to her about it," said he, "and your proposal made her
laugh; but I am sure she will make up her mind when she finds
herself in possession of the dress."

It was a Friday. The marquis sent in an excellent fish dinner,
and came himself soon after with the dress in a basket. The

present was made with all ceremony, and the proud countess was profuse in her expressions of thanks, which the giver received coolly enough, as if accustomed to that kind of thing. However, he ended by the no means flattering remark that if she had any sense she would sell it, as everybody knew she was too poor to wear it. This suggestion by no means met with her approval. She abused him to her heart's content, and told him he must be a great fool to give her a dress which he considered unsuitable to her.

They were disputing warmly when the Marchioness Menafoglio was announced. As soon as she came in her eyes were attracted by the dress, which was stretched over a chair, and finding it superb she exclaimed,

"I would gladly buy that dress."

"I did not buy it to sell again," said the countess, sharply.

"Excuse me," replied the marchioness, "I thought it was for sale, and I am sorry it is not."

The marquis, who was no lover of dissimulation, began to laugh, and the countess, fearing he would cover her with ridicule, hastened to change the conversation. But when the marchioness was gone the countess gave reins to her passion, and scolded the marquis bitterly for having laughed. However, he only replied by remarks which, though exquisitely polite, had a sting in them; and at last the lady said she was tired, and was going to lie down.

When she had left the room the marquis gave me the fifteen thousand francs, telling me that they would bring me good luck at Canano's.

"You are a great favourite of Canano's," he added, "and he wants you to come and dine with him. He can't ask you to supper, as he is obliged to spend his nights in the assembly-rooms."

"Tell him I will come any day he likes except the day after to-morrow, when I have to go to a wedding at the 'Apple Garden.'"

"I congratulate you," said the count and the marquis together, "it will no doubt be very pleasant."

"I expect to enjoy myself heartily there."

"Could not we come, too?"

"Do you really want to?"

"Certainly."

"Then I will get you an invitation from the fair bride herself on the condition that the countess comes as well. I must warn you that the company will consist of honest people of the lower classes, and I cannot have them humiliated in any way."

"I will persuade the countess," said Triulzi.

"To make your task an easier one, I may as well tell you that the wedding is that of the fair Zenobia."

"Bravo! I am sure the countess will come to that."

The count went out, and shortly reappeared with Zenobia. The marquis congratulated her, and encouraged her to ask the countess to the wedding. She seemed doubtful, so the marquis took her by the hand and let her into the proud Spaniard's room. In half an hour they returned informing us that my lady had deigned to accept the invitation.

When the marquis had gone, the count told me that I might go and keep his wife company, if I had nothing better to do, and that he would see to some business.

"I have the thousand sequins in my pocket," I remarked, "and if I find her reasonable, I will leave them with her."

"I will go and speak to her first."

"Do so."

While the count was out of the room, I exchanged the thousand sequins for the fifteen thousand francs in bank notes which Greppi had given me.

I was just shutting up my cash-box when Zenobia came in with my lace cuffs. She asked me if I would like to buy a piece of lace. I replied in the affirmative, and she went out and brought it me.

I liked the lace, and bought it for eighteen sequins, and said,—

"This lace is yours, dearest Zenobia, if you will content me this moment."

"I love you well, but I should be glad if you would wait till after my marriage."

"No, dearest, now or never. I cannot wait. I shall die if you do not grant my prayer. Look! do you not see what a state I am in?"

"I see it plainly enough, but it can't be done."

"Why not? Are you afraid of your husband noticing the loss of your maidenhead?"

"Not I, and if he did I shouldn't care. I promise you if he dared to reproach me, he should not have me at all."

"Well said, for my leavings are too good for him. Come quick!"

"But you will shut the door, at least?"

"No, the noise would be heard, and might give rise to suspicion. Nobody will come in."

With these words I drew her towards me, and finding her as gentle as a lamb and as loving as a dove, the amorous sacrifice was offered with abundant libations on both sides. After the first ecstacy was over, I proceeded to examine her beauties, and with my usual amorous frenzy told her that she should send her tailor out to graze and live with me. Fortunately she did not believe in the constancy of my passion. After a second assault I rested, greatly astonished that the count had not interrupted our pleasures. I thought he must have gone out, and I told Zenobia my opinion, whereon she overwhelmed me with caresses. Feeling at my ease, I set her free from her troublesome clothes, and gave myself up to toying with her in a manner calculated to arouse the exhausted senses; and then for the third time we were clasped to each other's arms, while I made Zenobia put herself into the many attitudes which I knew from experience as most propitious to the voluptuous triumph.

We were occupied a whole hour in these pleasures, but Zenobia, in the flower of her age and a novice, poured forth many more libations than I.

Just as I lost life for the third time, and Zenobia for the fourteenth, I heard the count's voice. I told my sweetheart, who had heard it as well, and after we had dressed hastily I gave her the eighteen sequins, and she left the room.

A moment after the count came in laughing, and said,—

"I have been watching you all the time by this chink" (which he shewed me), "and I have found it very amusing."

"I am delighted to hear it, but keep it to yourself."

"Of course, of course."

"My wife," said he, "will be very pleased to see you; and I," he added, "shall be very pleased as well."

"You are a philosophical husband," said I, "but I am afraid after the exercises you witnessed the countess will find me rather slow."

"Not at all, the recollection will make it all the pleasanter for you."

"Mentally perhaps, but in other respects . . ."

"Oh! you will manage to get out of it."

"My carriage is at your service, as I shall not be going out for the rest of the day."

I softly entered the countess's room and finding her in bed enquired affectionately after her health.

"I am very well," said she, smiling agreeably, "my husband has done me good."

I had seated myself quietly on the bed, and she had shewn no vexation; certainly a good omen.

"Aren't you going out any more to-day?" said she, "you have got your dressing-gown on."

"I fell asleep lying on my bed, and when I awoke I decided on keeping you company if you will be as good and gentle as you are pretty."

"If you behave well to me, you will always find me so.

"And will you love me?"

"That depends on you. So you are going to sacrifice Canano to me this evening."

"Yes, and with the greatest pleasure. He has won a lot from me already, and I foresee that he will win the fifteen thousand francs I have in my pocket to-morrow. This is the money the Marquis Triulzi gave me for the dress."

"It would be a pity to lose such a large sum."

"You are right, and I need not lose them if you will be complaisant, for they are meant for you. Allow me to shut the door."

"What for?"

"Because I am perishing with cold and desire, and intend warming myself in your bed."

"I will never allow that."

"I don't want to force you. Good-bye, countess, I will go and warm myself by my own fire, and to-morrow I will wage war on Canano's bank."

"You are certainly a sad dog. Stay here, I like your conversation."

Without more ado I locked the door, took off my clothes, and seeing that her back was turned to me, jumped into bed beside her. She had made up her mind, and let me do as I liked, but my combats with Zenobia had exhausted me. With closed eyes she let me place her in all the postures which lubricity could suggest, while her hands were not idle; but all was in vain, my torpor was complete, and nothing would give life to the instrument which was necessary to the operation.

Doubtless the Spaniard felt that my nullity was an insult to her charms; doubtless I must have tortured her by raising desires which I could not appease; for several times I felt my fingers drenched with a flow that shewed she was not passive in the matter; but she pretended all the while to be asleep. I was vexed at her being able to feign insensibility to such an extent, and I attached myself to her head; but her lips, which she abandoned to me, and which I abused disgracefully, produced no more effect than the rest of her body. I felt angry that I could not effect the miracle of resurrection, and I decided on leaving a stage where I had so wretched a part, but I was not generous to her, and put the finishing stroke to her humiliation by saying,—

"'Tis not my fault, madam, that your charms have so little power over me.
Here, take these fifteen thousand francs by way of consolation."

With this apostrophe I left her.

My readers, more especially my lady readers, if I ever have any, will no doubt pronounce me a detestable fellow after this. I understand their feelings, but beg them to suspend their judgment. They will see afterwards that my instinct served me wonderfully in the course I had taken.

Early the next day the count came into my room with a very pleased expression.

"My wife is very well," said he, "and told me to wish you good day."

I did not expect this, and I no doubt looked somewhat astonished.

"I am glad," he said, "that you gave her francs instead of the sequins you got from Triulzi, and I hope, as Triulzi said, you will have luck with it at the bank."

"I am not going to the opera," said I, "but to the masked ball, and I don't want anyone to recognize me."

I begged him to go and buy me a new domino, and not to come near me in the evening, so that none but he should know who I was. As soon as he had gone out I began to write letters. I had heavy arrears to make up in that direction.

The count brought me my domino at noon, and after hiding it we went to dine with the countess. Her affability, politeness, and gentleness astounded me. She looked so sweetly pretty that I repented having outraged her so scandalously. Her insensibility of the evening before seemed inconceivable, and I began to suspect that the signs I had noticed to the contrary were only due to the animal faculties which are specially active in sleep.

"Was she really asleep," said I to myself, "when I was outraging her so shamefully?"

I hoped it had been so. When her husband left us alone, I said, humbly and tenderly, that I knew I was a monster, and that she must detest me.

"You a monster?" said she. "On the contrary I owe much to you, and there is nothing I can think of for which I have cause to reproach you."

I took her hand, tenderly, and would have carried it to my lips, but she drew it away gently and gave me a kiss. My repentance brought a deep blush to my face.

When I got back to my room I sealed my letters and went to the ball. I was absolutely unrecognizable. Nobody had ever seen my watches or my snuff-boxes before, and I had even changed my purses for fear of anybody recognizing me by them.

Thus armed against the glances of the curious, I sat down at Canano's table and commenced to play in quite a different fashion. I had a hundred Spanish pieces in my pocket worth seven hundred Venetian sequins. I had got this Spanish money from Greppi, and I took care not to use what Triulzi had given me for fear he should know me.

I emptied my purse on the table, and in less than an hour it was all gone. I rose from the table and everybody thought I was going to beat a retreat, but I took out another purse and put a hundred sequins on one card, going second, with paroli, seven, and the va. The stroke was successful and Canano gave me back my hundred Spanish pieces, on which I sat down again by the banker, and recommenced regular play. Canano was looking at me hard. My snuff-box was the one which the Elector of Cologne had given me, with the prince's portrait on the lid. I took a pinch of snuff and he gave me to understand that he would like one too, and the box was subjected to a general examination. A lady whom I did not know said the portrait represented the Elector of Cologne in his robes as Grand Master of the Teutonic Order. The box was returned to me and I saw that it had made me respected, so small a thing imposes on people. I then put fifty sequins on one card, going paroli and paix de paroli, and at daybreak I had broken the bank. Canano said politely that if I liked to be spared the trouble of carrying all that gold he would have it weighed and give me a cheque. A pair of scales was brought, and it was found that I had thirty-four pounds weight in gold, amounting to two thousand eight hundred and fifty-six sequins. Canano wrote me a cheque, and I slowly returned to the ball-room.

Barbaro had recognized me with the keenness of a Venetian. He accosted me and congratulated me on my luck, but I gave him no answer, and seeing that I wished to remain incognito he left me.

A lady in a Greek dress richly adorned with diamonds came up to me, and said in a falsetto voice that she would like to dance with me.

I made a sign of assent, and as she took off her glove I saw a finely-shaped hand as white as alabaster, one of the fingers bearing an exquisite diamond ring. It was evidently no ordinary person, and though I puzzled my head I could not guess who she could be.

She danced admirably, in the style of a woman of fashion, and I too exerted myself to the utmost. By the time the dance was over I was covered with perspiration.

"You look hot," said my partner, in her falsetto voice, "come and rest in my box."

My heart leaped with joy, and I followed her with great delight; but as I saw Greppi in the box to which she took me, I had no doubt that it must be Therese, which did not please me quite so well. In short, the lady took off her mask; it was Therese, and I complimented her on her disguise.

"But how did you recognize me, dearest?"

"By your snuff-box. I knew it, otherwise I should never have found you out."

"Then you think that nobody has recognized me?"

"Nobody, unless in the same way as I did."

"None of the people here have seen my snuff-box."

I took the opportunity of handing over to Greppi Canano's cheque, and he gave me a receipt for it. Therese asked us to supper for the ensuing evening, and said,—

"There will be four of us in all."

Greppi seemed curious to know who the fourth person could be, but I right guessed it would be my dear son Cesarino.

As I went down once more to the ball-room two pretty female dominos attacked me right and left, telling me that Messer-Grande was waiting for me outside. They then asked me for some snuff, and I gave them a box ornamented with an indecent picture. I had the impudence to touch the spring and shew it them, and after inspecting it they exclaimed,—

"Fie, fie! your punishment is never to know who we are."

I was sorry to have displeased the two fair masquers, who seemed worth knowing, so I followed them, and meeting Barbaro, who knew everybody, I pointed them out to him, and heard to my delight that they were the two Marchionesses Q—— and F——. I promised Barbaro to go and see them. He said that everybody in the ball-room knew me, and that our bank was doing very well, though, of course, that was a trifle to me.

Towards the end of the ball, when it was already full daylight, a masquer, dressed as a Venetian gondolier, was accosted by a lady masquer, also in Venetian costume. She challenged the gondolier to prove himself a Venetian by dancing the 'forlana' with her. The gondolier accepted, and the music struck up, but the boatman, who was apparently a Milanese, was hooted, while the lady danced exquisitely. I was very fond of the dance, and I asked the unknown Venetian lady to dance it again with me. She agreed, and a ring was formed round us, and we were so applauded that we had to dance it over again. This would have sufficed if a very pretty shepherdess without a mask had not begged me to dance it with her. I could not refuse her, and she danced exquisitely; going round and round the circle three times, and seeming to hover in the air. I was quite out of breath. When it was finished, she came up to me and whispered my name in my ear. I was astonished, and feeling the charm of the situation demanded her name.

"You shall know," said she, in Venetian, "if you will come to the 'Three
Kings.'"

"Are you alone?"

"No, my father and mother, who are old friends of yours, are with me"

"I will call on Monday."

What a number of adventures to have in one night! I went home wearily, and went to bed, but I was only allowed to sleep for two hours. I was roused and begged to dress myself. The countess, the marquis, and the count, all ready for Zenobia's wedding, teased me till I was ready, telling me it was not polite to keep a bride waiting. Then they all congratulated me on my breaking the bank and the run of luck against me. I told the marquis that it was his money that had brought me luck, but he replied by saying that he knew what had become of his money.

This indiscretion either on the count's part or the countess's surprised me greatly; it seemed to me contrary to all the principles in intrigue.

"Canano knew you," said the marquis, "by the way you opened your snuff-box, and he hopes to see us to dinner before long. He says he hopes you will win a hundred pounds weight of gold; he has a fancy for you."

"Canano," said I, "has keen eyes, and plays faro admirably. I have not the slightest wish to win his money from him."

We then started for the "Apple Garden," where we found a score of honest folks and the bride and bridegroom, who overwhelmed us with compliments. We soon put the company at their ease. At first our presence overawed them, but a little familiarity soon restored the general hilarity. We sat down to dinner, and among the guests were some very pretty girls, but my head was too full of Zenobia to care about them. The dinner lasted three hours. It was an abundant repast, and the foreign wines were so exquisite that it was easy to see that the sum I had furnished had been exceeded. Good fellowship prevailed, and after the first bumper had passed round everybody proposed somebody else's health, and as each tried to say something different to his neighbour the most fearful nonsense prevailed. Then everybody thought himself bound to sing, and they were not at all first-rate vocalists by any means. We laughed heartily and also caused laughter, for our speeches and songs were as bad as those of our humble friends.

When we rose from the table kissing became general, and the countess could not resist laughing when she found herself obliged to hold out her cheeks for the salute of the tailor, who thought her laughter a special mark of favour.

Strains of sweet music were heard, and the ball was duly opened by the newly-married couple. Zenobia danced, if not exactly well, at least gracefully; but the tailor, who had never put his legs to any other use besides crossing them, cut such a ridiculous figure that the countess had much ado to restrain her laughter. But in spite of that I led out Zenobia for the next minuet, and the proud countess was obliged to dance with the wretched tailor.

When the minuets stopped the square dances began, and refreshments were liberally handed round. Confetti, a kind of sweetmeat, even better than that made at Verdun, were very plentiful.

When we were just going I congratulated the husband and offered to bring Zenobia home in my carriage, which he was pleased to style a very honourable offer. I gave my hand to Zenobia, and helped her into the carriage, and having told the coachman to go slowly I put her on my knee, extinguisher fashion, and kept her there all the time. Zenobia was the first to get down, and noticing that my breeches of grey velvet were spoiled, I told her that I would be with her in a few minutes. In two minutes I put on a pair of black satin breeches, and I rejoined the lady before her husband came in. She asked what I had been doing, and on my telling her that our exploits in the carriage had left very evident marks on my trousers, she gave me a kiss, and thanked me for my forethought.

Before long the husband and his sister arrived. He thanked me, calling me his gossip, and then noticing the change in my dress he asked me how I had contrived to make the alteration so quickly.

"I went to my room, leaving your wife at your house, for which I beg your pardon."

"Didn't you see that the gentleman had spilt a cup of coffee over his handsome breeches?" said Zenobia.

"My dear wife," said the crafty tailor, "I don't see everything, nor is it necessary that I should do so, but you should have accompanied the gentleman to his room."

Then turning to me with a laugh, he asked me how I had enjoyed the wedding.

"Immensely, and my friends have done the same; but you must let me pay you, dear gossip, for what you spent over and above the twenty-four sequins. You can tell me how much it is."

"Very little, a mere trifle; Zenobia shall bring you the bill."

I went home feeling vexed with myself for not having foreseen that the rogue would notice my change of dress, and guess the reason. However, I consoled myself with the thought that the tailor was no fool, and that it was plain that he was content to play the part we had assigned to him. So after wishing good night to the count, the countess and the marquis, who all thanked me for the happy day they had spent, I went to bed.

As soon as I was awake, I thought of the shepherdess who had danced the 'forlana' so well at the ball, and I resolved to pay her a visit. I was not more interested in her beauty than to find out who her father and mother, "old friends of mine," could be. I dressed and walked to the "Three Kings," and on walking into the room which the shepherdess had indicated to me, what was my astonishment to find myself face to face with the Countess Rinaldi, whom Zavoisky had introduced me to at the 'locanda' of Castelletto sixteen years ago. The reader will remember how M. de Bragadin paid her husband the money he won from me at play.

Madame Rinaldi had aged somewhat, but I knew her directly. However, as I had never had more than a passing fancy for her, we did not go back to days which did neither of us any honour.

"I am delighted to see you again," said I; "are you still living with your husband?"

"You will see him in half an hour, and he will be glad to present his respects to you."

"I should not at all care for it myself, madam; there are old quarrels between us which I do not want to renew, so, madam, farewell."

"No, no, don't go yet, sit down."

"Pardon me."

"Irene, don't let the gentleman go."

At these words Irene ran and barred the way—not like a fierce mastiff, but like an angel, entreating me to stay with that mingled look of innocence, fear, and hope, of which girls know the effect so well. I felt I could not go.

"Let me through, fair Irene," said I, "we may see each other somewhere else."

"Pray do not go before you have seen my father."

The words were spoken so tenderly that our lips met. Irene was victorious. How can one resist a pretty girl who implores with a kiss? I took a chair, and Irene, proud of her victory, sat on my knee and covered me with kisses.

I took it into my head to task the countess where and when Irene was born.

"At Mantua," said she, "three months after I left Venice."

"And when did you leave Venice?"

"Six months after I met you."

"That is a curious coincidence, and if we had been tenderly acquainted you might say that Irene was my daughter, and I should believe you, and think that my affection for her was purely paternal."

"Your memory is not very good, sir, I wonder at that."

"I may tell you, that I never forget certain things, But I guess your meaning. You want me to subdue my liking for Irene. I am willing to do so, but she will be the loser."

This conversation had silenced Irene, but she soon took courage, and said she was like me.

"No, no," I answered, "if you were like me you would not be so pretty."

"I don't think so; I think you are very handsome."

"You flatter me."

"Stay to dinner with us."

"No, if I stayed I might fall in love with you, and that would be a pity, as your mother says I am your father."

"I was joking," said the countess, "you may love Irene with a good conscience."

"We will see what can be done."

When Irene had left the room, I said to the mother,—

"I like your daughter, but I won't be long sighing for her, and you mustn't take me for a dupe."

"Speak to my husband about it. We are very poor, and we want to go to
Cremona."

"I suppose Irene has a lover?"

"No."

"But she has had one, of course?"

"Never anything serious."

"I can't believe it."

"It's true, nevertheless. Irene is intact."

Just then Irene came in with her father, who had aged to such an extent that I should never have known him in the street. He came up to me and embraced me, begging me to forget the past. "It is only you," he added, "who can furnish me with funds to go to Cremona.

"I have several debts here, and am in some danger of imprisonment. Nobody of any consequence comes to see me. My dear daughter is the only thing of value which I still possess. I have just been trying to sell this pinchbeck watch, and though I asked only six sequins, which is half what it is worth, they would not give me more than two. When a man gets unfortunate, everything is against him."

I took the watch, and gave the father six sequins for it, and then handed it to Irene. She said with a smile that she could not thank me, as I only gave her back her own, but she thanked me for the present I had made her father.

"Here," said she seriously to the old man, "you can sell it again now."

This made me laugh. I gave the count ten sequins in addition, embraced Irene, and said I must be gone, but that I would see them again in three or four days.

Irene escorted me to the bottom of the stairs, and as she allowed me to assure myself that she still possessed the rose of virginity, I gave her another ten sequins, and told her that the first time she went alone to the ball with me I would give her a hundred sequins. She said she would consult her father.

Feeling sure that the poor devil would hand over Irene to me, and having no apartment in which I could enjoy her in freedom, I stopped to read a bill in a pastrycook's window. It announced a room to let. I went in, and the pastrycook told me that the house belonged to him, and his pretty wife, who was suckling a baby, begged me to come upstairs and see the room. The street was a lonely one, and had a pleasing air of mystery about it. I climbed to the third floor, but the rooms there were wretched garrets of no use to me.

"The first floor," said the woman, "consists of a suite of four nice rooms, but we only let them together."

"Let us go and see them. Good! they will do. What is the rent?"

"You must settle that with my husband."

"And can't I settle anything with you, my dear?"

So saying I gave her a kiss which she took very kindly, but she smelt of nursing, which I detested, so I did not go any farther despite her radiant beauty.

I made my bargain with the landlord, and paid a month's rent in advance for which he gave me a receipt. It was agreed that I should come and go as I pleased, and that he should provide me with food. I gave him a name so common as to tell him nothing whatever about me, but he seemed to care very little about that.

As I had agreed with Barbaro to visit the fair marchionesses, I dressed carefully, and after a slight repast with the countess, who was pleasant but did not quite please me, I met my fellow-countryman and we called on the two cousins.

"I have come," said I, "to beg your pardons for having revealed to you the secret of the snuff-box."

They blushed, and scolded Barbaro, thinking that he had betrayed them. On examining them I found them far superior to Irene, my present flame, but their manner, the respect they seemed to require, frightened me. I was not at all disposed to dance attendance on them. Irene, on the contrary, was an easy prey. I had only to do her parents a service, and she was in my power; while the two cousins had their full share of aristocratic pride, which debases the nobility to the level of the vilest of the people, and only imposes upon fools, who after all are in the majority everywhere. Further I was no longer at that brilliant age which fears nothing, and I was afraid that my appearance would hardly overcome them. It is true that Barbaro had made me hope that presents would be of some use, but after what the Marquis Triulzi had said, I feared that Barbaro had only spoken on supposition.

When the company was sufficiently numerous, the card-tables were brought in. I sat down by Mdlle. Q——, and disposed myself to play for small stakes. I was introduced by the aunt, the mistress of the house, to a young gentleman in Austrian uniform who sat beside me.

My dear countryman played like a true sharper, much to my displeasure. My fair neighbour, at the end of the game, which lasted four hours, found herself the gainer of a few sequins, but the officer, who had played on his word of honour, after losing all the money in his pockets, owed ten louis. The bank was the winner of fifty sequins, including the officer's debt. As the young man lived at some distance he honoured me by coming in my carriage.

On the way, Barbaro told us he would introduce us to a girl who had just come from Venice. The officer caught fire at this, and begged that we should go and see her directly, and we accordingly went. The girl was well enough looking, but neither I nor the officer cared much about her. While they were making some coffee for us, and Barbaro was entertaining the young lady, I took a pack of cards, and had not much difficulty in inducing the officer to risk twenty sequins against the twenty I put on the table. While we were playing I spoke to him of the passion with which the young marchioness inspired me.

"She's my sister," said he.

I knew as much, but pretended to be astonished, and I went on playing. Taking the opportunity I told him that I knew of no one who could let the marchioness know of my affection better than he. I made him laugh, and as he thought I was jesting he only gave vague answers; but seeing that while I talked of my passion I forgot my card, he soon won the twenty sequins from me, and immediately paid them to Barbaro. In the excess of his joy he embraced me as if I had given him the money; and when we parted he promised to give me some good news of his sister at our next meeting.

I had to go to supper with Therese, Greppi, and my son, but having some spare time before me I went to the opera-house. The third act was going on, and I accordingly visited the cardroom, and there lost two hundred sequins at a single deal. I left the room almost as if I was flying from an enemy. Canano shook me by the hand, and told me he expected me and the marquis to dinner every day, and I promised we would come at the earliest opportunity.

I went to Therese's, and found Greppi there before me. Therese and Don Cesarino, whom I covered with kisses, came in a quarter of an hour afterwards. The banker stared at him in speechless wonder. He could not make out whether he was my son or my brother.

Seeing his amazement, Therese told him Cesarino was her brother. This stupefied the worthy man still more. At last he asked me if I had known Therese's mother pretty well, and on my answering in the affirmative he seemed more at ease.

The meal was excellent, but all my attention went to my son. He had all the advantages of a good disposition and an excellent education. He had grown a great deal since I had seen him at Florence, and his mental powers had developed proportionately. His presence made the party grave, but sweet. The innocence of youth throws around it an ineffable charm; it demands respect and restraint. An hour after midnight we left Therese, and I went to bed, well pleased with my day's work, for the loss of two hundred sequins did not trouble me much.

When I got up I received a note from Irene, begging me to call on her. Her father had given her permission to go to the next ball with me, and she had a domino, but she wanted to speak to me. I wrote and told her I would see her in the course of the day. I had written to tell the Marquis Triulzi that I was going to dine with Canano, and he replied that he would be there.

We found this skilled gamester in a fine house, richly furnished, and shewing traces on every side of the wealth and taste of its owner. Canano introduced me to two handsome women, one of whom was his mistress, and to five or six marquises; for at Milan no noble who is not a marquis is thought anything of, just as in the same way they are all counts at Vicenza. The dinner was magnificent and the conversation highly intellectual. In a mirthful moment Canano said he had known me for seventeen years, his acquaintance dating from the time I had juggled a professional gamester, calling himself Count Celi, out of a pretty ballet-girl whom I had taken to Mantua. I confessed the deed and amused the company by the story of what had happened at Mantua with Oreilan, and how I had found Count Celi at Cesena metamorphosed into Count Alfani. Somebody mentioned the ball which was to be held the next day, and when I said I was not going they laughed.

"I bet I know you," said Canano, "if you come to the bank."

"I am not going to play any more," said I.

"All the better for me," answered Canano; "for though your punting is unlucky, you don't leave off till you have won my money. But that's only my joke; try again, and I protest I would see you win half my fortune gladly."

Count Canano had a ring on his finger with a stone not unlike one of mine; it had cost him two thousand sequins, while mine was worth three thousand. He proposed that we should stake them against each other after having them unmounted and valued.

"When?" said I.

"Before going to the opera."

"Very good; but on two turns of the cards, and a deal to each."

"No, I never punt."

"Then we must equalise the game."

"How do you mean?"

"By leaving doubles and the last two cards out of account."

"Then you would have the advantage."

"If you can prove that I will pay you a hundred sequins. Indeed, I would bet anything you like that the game would still be to the advantage of the banker."

"Can you prove it?"

"Yes; and I will name the Marquis Triulzi as judge."

I was asked to prove my point without any question of a bet.

"The advantages of the banker," said I, "are two. The first and the smaller is that all he has got to attend to is not to deal wrongly, which is a very small matter to an habitual player; and all the time the punter has to rack his brains on the chances of one card or another coming out. The other advantage is one of time. The banker draws his card at least a second before the punter, and this again gives him a purchase."

No one replied; but after some thought the Marquis Triulzi said that to make the chances perfectly equal the players would have to be equal, which was almost out of the question.

"All that is too sublime for me," said Canano; "I don't understand it."
But, after all, there was not much to understand.

After dinner I went to the "Three Kings" to find out what Irene had to say to me, and to enjoy her presence. When she saw me she ran up to me, threw her arms round my neck, and kissed me, but with too much eagerness for me to lay much value on the salute. However, I have always known that if one wants to enjoy pleasure one must not philosophise about it, or one runs a risk of losing half the enjoyment. If Irene had struck me in dancing the 'forlana', why should not I have pleased her in spite of my superiority in age? It was not impossible, and that should be enough for me, as I did not intend to make her my wife.

The father and mother received me as their preserver, and they may have been sincere. The count begged me to come out of the room for a moment with him, and when we were on the other side of the door, said,—

"Forgive an old and unfortunate man, forgive a father, if I ask you whether it is true that you promised Irene a hundred sequins if I would let her go to the ball with you."

"It is quite true, but of course you know what the consequences will be."

At these words the poor old rascal took hold of me in a way which would have frightened me if I had not possessed twice his strength, but it was only to embrace me.

We went back to the room, he in tears and I laughing. He ran and told his wife, who had not been able to believe in such luck any more than her husband, and Irene added a comic element to the scene by saying,—

"You must not think me a liar, or that my parents suspected that I was imposing on them; they only thought you said fifty instead of a hundred, as if I were not worth such a sum."

"You are worth a thousand, my dear Irene; your courage in barring the way pleased me extremely. But you must come to the ball in a domino."

"Oh! you will be pleased with my dress."

"Are those the shoes and buckles you are going to wear? Have you no other stockings? Where are your gloves?"

"Good heavens! I have nothing."

"Quick! Send for the tradesmen. We will choose what we want, and I will pay."

Rinaldi went out to summon a jeweller, a shoemaker, a stocking-maker, and a perfumer. I spent thirty sequins in what I considered necessary, but then I noticed that there was no English point on her mask, and burst out again. The father brought in a milliner, who adorned the mask with an ell of lace for which I paid twelve sequins. Irene was in great delight, but her father and mother would have preferred to have the money in their pockets, and at bottom they were right.

When Irene put on her fine clothes I thought her delicious, and I saw what an essential thing dress is to a woman.

"Be ready," said I, "before the time for the opera to-morrow, for before going to the ball we will sup together in a room which belongs to me, where we shall be quite at our ease. You know what to expect," I added, embracing her. She answered me with an ardent kiss.

As I took leave of her father, he asked me where I was going after leaving Milan.

"To Marseilles, then to Paris, and then to London, at which place I intend stopping a year."

"Your flight from The Leads was wonderfully lucky."

"Yes, but I risked my life."

"You have certainly deserved all your good fortune."

"Do you think so? I have only used my fortune—in subservience to my pleasures."

"I wonder you do not have a regular mistress."

"The reason is, that I like to be my own master. A mistress at my coat-tails would be more troublesome than a wife; she would be an obstacle to the numerous pleasant adventures I encounter at every town. For example, if I had a mistress I should not be able to take the charming Irene to the ball to-morrow."

"You speak like a wise man."

"Yes, though my wisdom is by no means of the austere kind."

In the evening I went to the opera, and should no doubt have gone to the card-table if I had not seen Cesarino in the pit. I spent two delightful hours with him. He opened his heart to me, and begged me to plead for him with his sister to get her consent to his going to sea, for which he had a great longing. He said that he might make a large fortune by a judicious course of trading. After a temperate supper with my dear boy, I went to bed. The next morning the fine young officer, the Marchioness of Q——'s brother, came and asked me to give him a breakfast. He said he had communicated my proposal to his sister, and that she had replied that I must be making a fool of him, as it was not likely that a man who lived as I did would be thinking of marrying.

"I did not tell you that I aspired to the honour of marrying her."

"No, and I did not say anything about marriage; but that's what the girls are always aiming at."

"I must go and disabuse her of the notion."

"That's a good idea; principals are always the best in these affairs. Come at two o'clock, I shall be dining there, and as I have got to speak to her cousin you will be at liberty to say what you like."

This arrangement suited me exactly. I noticed that my future brother-in-law admired a little gold case on my night-table, so I begged him to accept it as a souvenir of our friendship. He embraced me, and put it in his pocket, saying he would keep it till his dying day.

"You mean till the day when it advances your suit with a lady," said I.

I was sure of having a good supper with Irene, so I resolved to take no dinner. As the count had gone to St. Angelo, fifteen miles from Milan, the day before, I felt obliged to wait on the countess in her room, to beg her to excuse my presence at dinner. She was very polite, and told me by no means to trouble myself. I suspected that she was trying to impose on me, but I wanted her to think she was doing so successfully. In my character of dupe I told her that in Lent I would make amends for the dissipation which prevented me paying my court to her. "Happily," I added, "Lent is not far off."

"I hope it will be so," said the deceitful woman with an enchanting smile, of which only a woman with poison in her heart is capable. With these words she took a pinch of snuff, and offered me her box.

"But what is this, my dear countess, it isn't snuff?"

"No," she replied, "it makes the nose bleed, and is an excellent thing for the head-ache."

I was sorry that I had taken it, but said with a laugh, that I had not got a head-ache, and did not like my nose to bleed.

"It won't bleed much," said she, with a smile, "and it is really beneficial."

As she spoke, we both began to sneeze, and I should have felt very angry if I had not seen her smile.

Knowing something about these sneezing powders, I did not think we should bleed, but I was mistaken. Directly after, I felt a drop of blood, and she took a silver basin from her night-table.

"Come here," said she, "I am beginning to bleed too."

There we were, bleeding into the same basin, facing each other in the most ridiculous position. After about thirty drops had fallen from each of us, the bleeding ceased. She was laughing all the time, and I thought the best thing I could do was to imitate her example. We washed ourselves in fair water in another basin.

"This admixture of our blood," said she, still smiling, "will create a sweet sympathy between us, which will only end with the death of one or the other."

I could make no sense of this, but the reader will soon see that the wretched woman did not mean our friendship to last very long. I asked her to give me some of the powder, but she refused; and on my enquiring the name of it, she replied that she did not know, as a lady friend had given it to her.

I was a good deal puzzled by the effects of this powder, never having heard of the like before, and as soon as I left the countess I went to an apothecary to enquire about it, but Mr. Drench was no wiser than I. He certainly said that euphorbia sometimes produced bleeding of the nose, but it was not a case of sometimes but always. This small adventure made me think seriously. The lady was Spanish, and she must hate me; and these two facts gave an importance to our blood-letting which it would not otherwise possess.

I went to see the two charming cousins, and I found the young officer with Mdlle. F—— in the room by the garden. The lady was writing, and on the pretext of not disturbing her I went after Mdlle. Q——, who was in the garden. I greeted her politely, and said I had come to apologize for a stupid blunder which must have given her a very poor opinion of me.

"I guess what you mean, but please to understand that my brother gave me your message in perfect innocence. Let him believe what he likes. Do you think I really believed you capable of taking such a step, when we barely knew each other?"

"I am glad to hear you say so."

"I thought the best thing would be to give a matrimonial turn to your gallantry. Otherwise my brother, who is quite a young man, might have interpreted it in an unfavourable sense."

"That was cleverly done, and of course I have nothing more to say. Nevertheless, I am 'grateful to your brother for having given you to understand that your charms have produced a vivid impression on me. I would do anything to convince you of my affection.."

"That is all very well, but it would have been wiser to conceal your feelings from my brother, and, allow me to add, from myself as well. You might have loved me without telling me, and then, though I should have perceived the state of your affections, I could have pretended not to do so. Then I should have been at my ease, but as circumstances now stand I shall have to be careful. Do you see?"

"Really, marchioness, you astonish me. I was never so clearly convinced that I have done a foolish thing. And what is still more surprising, is that I was aware of all you have told me. But you have made me lose my head. I hope you will not punish me too severely?"

"Pray inform me how it lies in my power to punish you."

"By not loving me."

"Ah! loving and not loving; that is out of one's power. Of a sudden we know that we are in love, and our fate is sealed."

I interpreted these last words to my own advantage, and turned the conversation. I asked her if she was going to the ball.

"No."

"Perhaps you are going incognito?"

"We should like to, but it is an impossibility; there is always someone who knows us."

"If you would take me into your service, I would wager anything that you would not be recognized."

"You would not care to trouble yourself about us."

"I like you to be a little sceptical, but put me to the proof. If you could manage to slip out unobserved, I would engage to disguise you in such a manner that no one would know you."

"We could leave the house with my brother and a young lady with whom he is in love. I am sure he would keep our counsel."

"I shall be delighted, but it must be for the ball on Sunday. I will talk it over with your brother. Kindly warn him not to let Barbaro know anything about it. You will be able to put on your disguise in a place I know of. However, we can settle about that again. I shall carry the matter through, you may be sure, with great secrecy. Permit me to kiss your hand."

She gave it me, and after imprinting a gentle kiss I held it to my heart, and had the happiness of feeling a soft pressure. I had no particular disguise in my head, but feeling sure of hitting on something I put off the consideration of it till the next day; the present belonged to Irene. I put on my domino, and went to the "Three Kings," where I found Irene waiting for me at the door. She had run down as soon as she had seen my carriage, and I was flattered by this mark of her eagerness. We went to my rooms, and I ordered the confectioner to get me a choice supper by midnight. We had six hours before us, but the reader will excuse my describing the manner in which they were spent. The opening was made with the usual fracture, which Irene bore with a smile, for she was naturally voluptuous. We got up at midnight, pleasantly surprised to find ourselves famishing with hunger, and a delicious supper waiting for us.

Irene told me that her father had taught her to deal in such a manner that she could not lose. I was curious to see how it was done, and on my giving her a pack of cards she proceeded to distract my attention by talking to me, and in a few minutes the thing was done. I gave her the hundred sequins I had promised her, and told her to go on with her play.

"If you only play on a single card," said she, "you are sure to lose."

"Never mind; go ahead."

She did so, and I was forced to confess that if I had not been warned I should never have detected the trick. I saw what a treasure she must be to the old rascal Rinaldi. With her air of innocence and gaiety, she would have imposed on the most experienced sharpers. She said in a mortified manner that she never had any opportunity of turning her talents to account, as their associates were always a beggarly lot. She added tenderly that if I would take her with me she would leave her parents there and win treasures for me.

"When I am not playing against sharpers," she said, "I can also punt very well."

"Then you can come to Canano's bank and risk the hundred sequins I have given you. Put twenty sequins on a card, and if you win go paroli, seven, and the va, and leave the game when they turn up. If you can't make the three cards come out second, you will lose, but I will reimburse you."

At this she embraced me, and asked if I would take half the profits.

"No," said I, "you shall have it all."

I thought she would have gone mad with joy.

We went off in sedan-chairs, and the ball not having commenced we went to the assembly-rooms. Canano had not yet done anything, and he opened a pack of cards and pretended not to recognize me, but he smiled to see the pretty masker, my companion, sit down and play instead of me. Irene made him a profound bow as he made room for her by his side, and putting the hundred sequins before her she began by winning a hundred and twenty-five, as instead of going seven and the va, she only went the paix de paroli. I was pleased to see her thus careful, and I let her go on. In the following deal she lost on three cards in succession, and then won another paix de paroli. She then bowed to the banker, pocketed her winnings, and left the table, but just as we were going out I heard somebody sobbing, and on my turning to her she said,

"I am sure it is my father weeping for joy."

She had three hundred and sixty sequins which she took to him after amusing herself for a few hours. I only danced one minuet with her, for my amorous exploits and the heavy supper I had taken had tired me, and I longed for rest. I let Irene dance with whom she liked, and going into a corner fell asleep. I woke up with a start and saw Irene standing before me. I had been asleep for three hours. I took her back to the "Three Kings," and left her in the charge of her father and mother. The poor man was quite alarmed to see so much gold on the table, and told me to wish him a pleasant journey, as he was starting in a few hours. I could make no opposition and I did not wish to do so, but Irene was furious.

"I won't go," she cried; "I want to stay with my lover. You are the ruin of my life. Whenever anybody takes a liking to me, you snatch me away. I belong to this gentleman, and I won't leave him."

However, she saw that I did not back her up, and began to weep, then kissed me again and again, and just as she was going to sit down, worn out with fatigue and despair, I went off, wishing them a pleasant journey, and telling Irene we should meet again. The reader will learn in due time when and how I saw them again. After all the fatigue I had gone through I was glad to go to bed.

It was eight o'clock when the young lieutenant awoke me.

"My sister has told me about the masquerade," said he, "but I have a great secret to confide in you."

"Say on, and count on my keeping your secret."

"One of the finest noblemen of the town, my friend and my cousin's lover, who has to be very careful of his actions on account of his exalted position, would like to be of the party if you have no objection. My sister and my cousin would like him to come very much."

"Of course he shall. I have been making my calculations for a party of five, and now it will be a party of six, that is all."

"You really are a splendid fellow."

"On Sunday evening you must be at a certain place, of which I will tell you. First of all we will have supper, then put on our disguises, and then go to the ball. To-morrow at five o'clock we shall meet at your sister's. All I want to know is what is the height of your mistress and of the young nobleman."

"My sweetheart is two inches shorter than my sister, and a little thinner; my friend is just about the same make as you are, and if you were dressed alike you would be mistaken for each other."

"That will do. Let me think it over, and leave me alone now; there's a
Capuchin waiting for me, and I am curious to learn his business."

A Capuchin had called on me and I had told Clairmont to give him an alms, but he had said he wanted to speak to me in private. I was puzzled, for what could a Capuchin have to say to me?

He came in, and I was at once impressed by his grave and reverend appearance. I made him a profound bow and offered him a seat, but he remained standing, and said,

"Sir, listen attentively to what I am about to tell you, and beware of despising my advice, for it might cost you your life. You would repent when it was too late. After hearing me, follow my advice immediately; but ask no questions, for I can answer none. You may guess, perhaps, that what silences me is a reason incumbent on all Christians—the sacred seal of the confessional. You may be sure that my word is above suspicion; I have no interests of my own to serve. I am acting in obedience to an inspiration; I think it must be your guardian angel speaking with my voice. God will not abandon you to the malice of your enemies. Tell me if I have touched your heart, and if you feel disposed to follow the counsels I am going to give you."

"I have listened to you, father, with attention and respect. Speak freely and advise me; what you have said has not only moved me, but has almost frightened me. I promise to do as you tell me if it is nothing against honour or the light of reason."

"Very good. A feeling of charity will prevent your doing anything to compromise me, whatever may be the end of the affair. You will not speak of me to anyone, or say either that you know me or do not know me?"

"I swear to you I will not on my faith as a Christian. But speak, I entreat you. Your long preface has made me burn with impatience."

"This day, before noon, go by yourself to—— Square, No.—-, on the second floor, and ring at the bell on your left. Tell the person who opens the door that you want to speak to Madame. You will be taken to her room without any difficulty; I am sure your name will not be asked, but if they do ask you, give an imaginary name. When you are face to face with the woman, beg her to hear you, and ask her for her secret, and to inspire confidence put a sequin or two in her hand. She is poor, and I am sure that your generosity will make her your friend. She will shut her door, and tell you to say on.

"You must then look grave, and tell her that you are not going to leave her house before she gives you the little bottle that a servant brought her yesterday with a note. If she resists, remain firm, but make no noise; do not let her leave the room or call anybody. Finally, tell her that you will give her double the money she may lose by giving you the bottle and all that depends on it. Remember these words: and all that depends on it. She will do whatever you want. It will not cost you much, but even if it did, your life is worth more than all the gold of Peru. I can say no more, but before I go, promise me that you will follow my advice."

"Yes, reverend father, I will follow the inspiration of the angel who led you here."

"May God give you His blessing."

When the good priest went out I did not feel at all disposed to laugh. Reason, certainly, bade me despise the warning, but my inherent superstition was too strong for reason. Besides, I liked the Capuchin. He looked like a good man, and I felt bound by the promise I had given him. He had persuaded me, and my reason told me that a man should never go against his persuasion; in fine, I had made up my mind. I took the piece of paper on which I had written the words I had to use, I put a pair of pistols in my pocket, and I told Clairmont to wait for me in the square. This latter, I thought, was a precaution that could do no harm.

Everything happened as the good Capuchin had said. The awful old creature took courage at the sight of the two sequins, and bolted her door. She began by laughing and saying that she knew I was amorous, and that it was my fault if I were not happy, but that she would do my business for me. I saw by these words that I had to do with a pretended sorceress. The famous Mother Bontemps had spoken in the same way to me at Paris. But when I told her that I was not going to leave the room till I had got the mysterious bottle, and all that depended on it, her face became fearful; she trembled, and would have escaped from the room; but I stood before her with an open knife, and would not suffer her to pass. But on my telling her that I would give her double the sum she was to be paid for her witchcraft, and that thus she would be the gainer and not a loser in complying with my demands, she became calm once more.

"I shall lose six sequins," said she, "but you will gladly pay double when I shew you what I have got; I know who you are."

"Who am I?"

"Giacomo Casanova, the Venetian."

It was then I drew the ten sequins from my purse. The old woman was softened at the sight of the money, and said,

"I would not have killed you outright, certainly, but I would have made you amorous and wretched."

"Explain what you mean."

"Follow me."

I went after her into a closet, and was greatly amazed at sing numerous articles about which my common sense could tell me nothing. There were phials of all shapes and sizes, stones of different colours, metals, minerals, big nails and small nails, pincers, crucibles, misshapen images, and the like.

"Here is the bottle," said the old woman.

"What does it contain?"

"Your blood and the countess's, as you will see in this letter."

I understood everything then, and now I wonder I did not burst out laughing. But as a matter of fact my hair stood on end, as I reflected on the awful wickedness of which the Spaniard was capable. A cold sweat burst out all over my body.

"What would you have done with this blood?"

"I should have plastered you with it."

"What do you mean by 'plastered'? I don't understand you."

"I will shew you."

As I trembled with fear the old woman opened a casket, a cubit long, containing a waxen statue of a man lying on his back. My name was written on it, and though it was badly moulded, my features were recognizable. The image bore my cross of the Order of the Golden Spur, and the generative organs were made of an enormous size. At this I burst into a fit of hysterical laughter, and had to sit down in an arm-chair till it was over.

As soon as I had got back my breath the sorceress said,

"You laugh, do you? Woe to you if I had bathed you in the bath of blood mingled according to my art, and more woe still if, after I had bathed you, I had thrown your image on a burning coal."

"Is this all?"

"Yes."

"All the apparatus is to become mine for twelve sequins; here they are. And now, quick! light me a fire that I may melt this monster, and as for the blood I think I will throw it out of the window."

This was no sooner said than done.

The old woman had been afraid that I should take the bottle and the image home with me, and use them to her ruin; and she was delighted to see me melt the image. She told me that I was an angel of goodness, and begged me not to tell anyone of what had passed between us. I swore I would keep my own counsel, even with the countess.

I was astonished when she calmly offered to make the countess madly in love with me for another twelve sequins, but I politely refused and advised her to abandon her fearful trade if she did not want to be burnt alive.

I found Clairmont at his post, and I sent him home. In spite of all I had gone through, I was not sorry to have acquired the information, and to have followed the advice of the good Capuchin who really believed me to be in deadly peril. He had doubtless heard of it in the confessional from the woman who had carried the blood to the witch. Auricular confession often works miracles of this kind.

I was determined never to let the countess suspect that I had discovered her criminal project, and I resolved to behave towards her so as to appease her anger, and to make her forget the cruel insult to which I had subjected her. It was lucky for me that she believed in sorcery; otherwise she would have had me assassinated.

As soon as I got in, I chose the better of the two cloaks I had, and presented her with it. She accepted the gift with exquisite grace, and asked me why I gave it her.

"I dreamt," said I, "that you were so angry with me that you were going to have me assassinated."

She blushed, and answered that she had not gone mad. I left her absorbed in a sombre reverie. Nevertheless, whether she forgot and forgave, or whether she could hit upon no other way of taking vengeance, she was perfectly agreeable to me during the rest of my stay in Milan.

The count came back from his estate, and said that we must really go and see the place at the beginning of Lent. I promised I would come, but the countess said she could not be of the party. I pretended to be mortified, but in reality her determination was an extremely pleasant one to me.

CHAPTER XX.

The Masquerade—My Amour with the Fair Marchioness—The Deserted Girl; I
Become Her Deliverer—My Departure for St. Angelo

As I had engaged myself to provide an absolutely impenetrable disguise, I wanted to invent a costume remarkable at once for its originality and its richness. I tortured my brains so to speak, and my readers shall see if they think my invention was a good one.

I wanted someone on whom I could rely, and above all, a tailor. It may be imagined that my worthy gossip was the tailor I immediately thought of. Zenobia would be as serviceable as her husband; she could do some of the work, and wait on the young ladies whom I was going to dress up.

I talked to my gossip, and told him to take me to the best second-hand clothes dealer in Milan.

When we got to the shop I said to the man—

"I want to look at your very finest costumes, both for ladies and gentlemen."

"Would you like something that has never been worn?"

"Certainly, if you have got such a thing."

"I have a very rich assortment of new clothes."

"Get me, then, in the first place, a handsome velvet suit, all in one piece, which nobody in Milan will be able to recognize."

Instead of one he shewed me a dozen such suits, all in excellent condition. I chose a blue velvet lined with white satin. The tailor conducted the bargaining, and it was laid on one side; this was for the pretty cousin's lover. Another suit, in smooth sulphur-coloured velvet throughout, I put aside for the young officer. I also took two handsome pairs of trousers in smooth velvet, and two superb silk vests.

I then chose two dresses, one flame-coloured and the other purple, and a third dress in shot silk. This was for the officer's mistress. Then came lace shirts, two for men, and three for women, then lace handkerchiefs, and finally scraps of velvet, satin, shot silk, etc., all of different colours.

I paid two hundred gold ducats for the lot, but on the condition that if anybody came to know that I had bought them by any indiscretion of his he should give me the money and take back the materials in whatever condition they might be in. The agreement was written out and signed, and I returned with the tailor, who carried the whole bundle to my rooms over the pastrycook's.

When it was all spread out on the table I told the tailor that I would blow out his brains if he told anybody about it, and then taking a stiletto I proceeded to cut and slash the coats, vests, and trousers all over, to the astonishment of the tailor, who thought I must be mad to treat such beautiful clothes in this manner.

After this operation, which makes me laugh to this day when I remember it, I took the scraps I had bought and said to the tailor,—

"Now, 'gossip, it is your turn; I want you to sew in these pieces into the holes I have made, and I hope your tailoring genius will aid you to produce some pretty contrasts. You see that you have got your work cut out for you and no time to lose. I will see that your meals are properly served in an adjoining chamber, but you must not leave the house till the work is finished. I will go for your wife, who will help you, and you can sleep together."

"For God's sake, sir! you don't want the ladies' dresses treated like the coats and trousers?"

"Just the same."

"What a pity! it will make my wife cry."

"I will console her."

On my way to Zenobia's I bought five pairs of white silk stockings, men's and women's gloves, two fine castor hats, two burlesque men's masks, and three graceful-looking female masks. I also bought two pretty china plates, and I carried them all to Zenobia's in a sedan-chair.

I found that charming woman engaged in her toilet. Her beautiful tresses hung about her neck, and her full breast was concealed by no kerchief. Such charms called for my homage, and to begin with I devoured her with kisses. I spent half an hour with her, and my readers will guess that it was well employed. I then helped her to finish her toilette, and we went off in the sedan-chair.

We found the tailor engaged in picking out the scraps and cutting them to fit the holes I had made. Zenobia looked on in a kind of stupor, and when she saw me begin to slash the dresses she turned pale and made an involuntary motion to stay my hand, for not knowing my intentions she thought I must be beside myself. Her husband had got hardened, and reassured her, and when she heard my explanation she became calm, though the idea struck her as a very odd one.

When it is a question of an affair of the heart, of the passions, or of pleasure, a woman's fancy moves much faster than a man's. When Zenobia knew that these dresses were meant for three beautiful women, whom I wished to make a centre of attraction to the whole assembly, she improved on my cuts and slashes, and arranged the rents in such a manner that they would inspire passion without wounding modesty. The dresses were slashed especially at the breast, the shoulders, and the sleeves; so that the lace shift could be seen, and in its turn the shift was cut open here and there, and the sleeves were so arranged that half the arms could be seen. I saw sure that she understood what I wanted, and that she would keep her husband right; and I left them, encouraging them to work their best and quickest. But I looked in three or four times in the day, and was more satisfied every time with my idea and their execution.

The work was not finished till the Saturday afternoon. I gave the tailor six sequins and dismissed him, but I kept Zenobia to attend on the ladies. I took care to place powder, pomade, combs, pins, and everything that a lady needs, on the table, not forgetting ribbons and pack-thread.

The next day I found play going on in a very spirited manner, but the two cousins were not at the tables, so I went after them. They told me they had given up playing as Barbaro always won.

"You have been losing, then?"

"Yes, but my brother has won something," said the amiable Q——.

"I hope luck will declare itself on your side also."

"No, we are not lucky."

When their aunt left the room, they asked me if the lieutenant had told me that a lady friend of theirs was coming to the ball with them.

"I know all," I answered, "and I hope you will enjoy yourselves, but you will not do so more than I. I want to speak to the gallant lieutenant to-morrow morning."

"Tell us about our disguises."

"You will be disguised in such a manner that nobody will recognize you."

"But how shall we be dressed?"

"Very handsomely."

"But what costume have you given us?"

"That is my secret, ladies. However much I should like to please you, I shall say nothing till the time for you to dress comes round. Don't ask me anything more, as I have promised myself the enjoyment of your surprise. I am very fond of dramatic situations. You shall know all after supper."

"Are we to have supper, then?"

"Certainly, if you would like it. I am a great eater myself and I hope you will not let me eat alone."

"Then we will have some supper to please you. We will take care not to eat much dinner, so as to be able to vie with you in the evening. The only thing I am sorry about," added Mdlle. Q——, "is that you should be put to such expense."

"It is a pleasure; and when I leave Milan I shall console myself with the thought that I have supped with the two handsomest ladies in the town."

"How is fortune treating you?"

"Canano wins two hundred sequins from me every day."

"But you won two thousand from him in one night."

"You will break his bank on Sunday. We will bring you luck."

"Would you like to look on?"

"We should be delighted, but my brother says you don't want to go with us."

"Quite so, the reason is that I should be recognized. But I believe the gentleman who will accompany you is of the same figure as myself."

"Exactly the same," said the cousin; "except that he is fair."

"All the better," said I, "the fair always conquer the dark with ease."

"Not always," said the other. "But tell us, at any rate, whether we are to wear men's dresses."

"Fie! fie! I should be angry with myself if I had entertained such a thought."

"That's curious; why so?"

"I'll tell you. If the disguise is complete I am disgusted, for the shape of a woman is much more marked than that of a man, and consequently a woman in man's dress, who looks like a man, cannot have a good figure."

"But when a woman skews her shape well?"

"Then I am angry with her for skewing too much, for I like to see the face and the general outlines of the form and to guess the rest."

"But the imagination is often deceptive!"

"Yes, but it is with the face that I always fall in love, and that never deceives me as far as it is concerned. Then if I have the good fortune to see anything more I am always in a lenient mood and disposed to pass over small faults. You are laughing?"

"I am smiling at your impassioned arguments."

"Would you like to be dressed like a man?"

"I was expecting something of the kind, but after you have said we can make no more objections."

"I can imagine what you would say; I should certainly not take you for men, but I will say no more."

They looked at each other, and blushed and smiled as they saw my gaze fixed on two pre-eminences which one would never expect to see in any man. We began to talk of other things, and for two hours I enjoyed their lively and cultured conversation.

When I left them I went off to my apartments, then to the opera, where I lost two hundred sequins, and finally supped with the countess, who had become quite amiable. However, she soon fell back into her old ways when she found that my politeness was merely external, and that I had no intentions whatever of troubling her in her bedroom again.

On the Saturday morning the young officer came to see me, and I told him that there was only one thing that I wanted him to do, but that it must be done exactly according to my instructions. He promised to follow them to the letter, and I proceeded,—

"You must get a carriage and four, and as soon as the five of you are in it tell the coachman to drive as fast as his horses can gallop out of Milan, and to bring you back again by another road to the house. There you must get down, send the carriage away, after enjoining silence on the coachman, and come in. After the ball you will undress in the same house, and then go home in sedan-chairs. Thus we shall be able to baffle the inquisitive, who will be pretty numerous, I warn you."

"My friend the marquis will see to all that," said he, "and I promise you he will do it well, for he is longing to make your acquaintance."

"I shall expect you, then, at seven o'clock to-morrow.

"Warn your friend that it is important the coachman should not be known, and do not let anybody bring a servant."

All these arrangements being made, I determined to disguise myself as Pierrot. There's no disguise more perfect; for, besides concealing the features and the shape of the body, it does not even let the colour of the skin remain recognizable. My readers may remember what happened to me in this disguise ten years before. I made the tailor get me a new Pierrot costume, which I placed with the others, and with two new purses, in each of which I placed five hundred sequins, I repaired to the pastrycook's before seven o'clock. I found the table spread, and the supper ready. I shut up Zenobia in the room where the ladies were to make their toilette, and at five minutes past seven the joyous company arrived.

The marquis was delighted to make my acquaintance, and I welcomed him as he deserved. He was a perfect gentleman in every respect, handsome, rich, and young, very much in love with the pretty cousin whom he treated with great respect. The lieutenant's mistress was a delightful little lady and madly fond of her lover.

As they were all aware that I did not want them to know their costumes till after supper, nothing was said about it, and we sat down to table. The supper was excellent; I had ordered it in accordance with my own tastes; that is to say, everything was of the best, and there was plenty of everything. When we had eaten and drunk well, I said,—

"As I am not going to appear with you, I may as well tell you the parts you are to play. You are to be five beggars, two men and three women, all rags and tatters."

The long faces they pulled at this announcement were a pleasant sight to see.

"You will each carry a plate in your hands to solicit alms, and you must walk together about the ball-room as a band of mendicants. But now follow me and take possession of your ragged robes."

Although I had much ado to refrain from laughing at the vexation and disappointment which appeared on all their faces, I succeeded in preserving my serious air. They did not seem in any kind of hurry to get their clothes, and I was obliged to tell them that they were keeping me waiting. They rose from the table and I threw the door open, and all were struck with Zenobia's beauty as she stood up by the table on which the rich though tattered robes were displayed, bowing to the company with much grace.

"Here, ladies," said I to the cousins, "are your dresses, and here is yours, mademoiselle—a little smaller. Here are your shifts, your handkerchiefs and your stockings, and I think you will find everything you require on this table. Here are masks, the faces of which shew so poorly beside your own, and here are three plates to crave alms. If anybody looks as high as your garters, they will see how wretched you are, and the holes in the stockings will let people know that you have not the wherewithal to buy silk to mend them. This packthread must serve you for buckles, and we must take care that there are holes in your shoes and also in your gloves, and as everything must match, as soon as you have put on your chemises you must tear the lace round the neck."

While I was going through this explanation I saw surprise and delight efface the disappointment and vexation which had been there a moment before. They saw what a rich disguise I had provided for them, and they could not find it in their hearts to say, "What a pity!"

"Here, gentlemen, are your beggar-clothes. I forgot to lacerate your beaver hats, but that is soon done. Well, what do you think of the costume?"

"Now, ladies, we must leave you; shut the door fast, for it is a case of changing your shifts. Now, gentlemen, leave the room."

The marquis was enthusiastic.

"What a sensation we shall create!" said he, "nothing could be better."

In half an hour we were ready. The stockings in holes, the worn-out shoes, the lace in rags, the straggling hair, the sad masks, the notched plates—all made a picture of sumptuous misery hard to be described.

The ladies took more time on account of their hair, which floated on their shoulders in fine disorder. Mdlle. Q——'s hair was especially fine, it extended almost to her knees.

When they were ready the door was opened, and we saw everything which could excite desire without wounding decency. I admired Zenobia's adroitness. The rents in dresses and chemises disclosed parts of their shoulders, their breasts, and their arms, and their white legs shone through the holes in the stockings.

I shewed them how to walk, and to sway their heads to and fro, to excite compassion, and yet be graceful, and how to use their handkerchiefs to shew people the tears in them and the fineness of the lace. They were delighted, and longed to be at the ball, but I wanted to be there first to have the pleasure of seeing them come in. I put on my mask, told Zenobia to go to bed, as we would not be back till daybreak, and set out on my way.

I entered the ball-room, and as there were a score of Pierrots nobody noticed me. Five minutes after there was a rush to see some maskers who were coming in, and I stood so as to have a good view. The marquis came in first between the two cousins. Their slow, pitiful step matched the part wonderfully. Mdlle. Q—— with her flame-coloured dress, her splendid hair, and her fine shape, drew all eyes towards her. The astonished and inquisitive crowd kept silence for a quarter of an hour after they had come in, and then I heard on every side, "What a disguise!" "It's wonderful!" "Who are they?" "Who can they be?" "I don't know." "I'll find out."

I enjoyed the results of my inventiveness.

The music struck up, and three fine dominos went up to the three beggar-girls to ask them to dance a minuet, but they excused themselves by pointing to their dilapidated shoes. I was delighted; it shewed that they had entered into the spirit of the part.

I followed them about for a quarter of an hour, and the curiosity about them only increased, and then I paid a visit to Canano's table, where play was running high. A masquer dressed in the Venetian style was punting on a single card, going fifty sequins paroli and paix de paroli, in my fashion. He lost three hundred sequins, and as he was a man of about the same size as myself people said it was Casanova, but Canano would not agree. In order that I might be able to stay at the table, I took up the cards and punted three or four ducats like a beginner. The next deal the Venetian masquer had a run of luck, and going paroli, paix de paroli and the va, won back all the money he had lost.

The next deal was also in his favour, and he collected his winnings and left the table.

I sat down in the chair he had occupied, and a lady said,—

"That's the Chevalier de Seingalt."

"No," said another. "I saw him a little while ago in the ball-room disguised as a beggar, with four other masquers whom nobody knows."

"How do you mean, dressed as a beggar?" said Canano.

"Why, in rags, and the four others, too; but in spite of that the dresses are splendid and the effect is very good. They are asking for alms."

"They ought to be turned out," said another.

I was delighted to have attained my object, for the recognition of me was a mere guess. I began putting sequins on one card, and I lost five or six times running. Canano studied me, but I saw he could not make me out. I heard whispers running round the table.

"It isn't Seingalt; he doesn't play like that; besides, he is at the ball."

The luck turned; three deals were in my favour, and brought me back more than I had lost. I continued playing with a heap of gold before me, and on my putting a fistfull of sequins on a card it came out, and I went paroli and pair de paroli. I won again, and seeing that the bank was at a low ebb I stopped playing. Canano paid me, and told his cashier to get a thousand sequins, and as he was shuffling the cards I heard a cry of, "Here come the beggars."

The beggars came in and stood by the table, and Canano, catching the marquis's eye, asked him for a pinch of snuff. My delight may be imagined when I saw him modestly presenting a common horn snuffbox to the banker. I had not thought of this detail, which made everybody laugh immensely. Mdlle. Q——stretched out her plate to ask an alms of Canano, who said,—

"I don't pity you with that fine hair of yours, and if you like to put it on a card I will allow you a thousand sequins for it."

She gave no answer to this polite speech, and held out her plate to me, and I put a handful of sequins on it, treating the other beggars in the same way.

"Pierrot seems to like beggars," said Canano, with a smile.

The three mendicants bowed gratefully to me and left the room.

The Marquis Triulzi who sat near Canano, said,—

"The beggar in the straw-coloured dress is certainly Casanova."

"I recognized him directly," replied the banker, "but who are the others?"

"We shall find out in due time."

"A dearer costume could not be imagined; all the dresses are quite new."

The thousand sequins came in, and I carried them all off in two deals.

"Would you like to go on playing?" said Canano.

I shook my head, and indicating with a sign of my hand that I would take a cheque, he weighed my winnings and gave me a cheque for twenty-nine pounds of gold, amounting to two thousand, five hundred sequins. I put away the cheque, and after shaking him by the hand, I got up and rolled away in true Pierrot fashion, and after making the tour of the ball-room I went to a box on the third tier of which I had given the key to the young officer, and there I found my beggars.

We took off our masks and congratulated each other on our success, and told our adventures. We had nothing to fear from inquisitive eyes, for the boxes on each side of us were empty. I had taken them myself, and the keys were in my pocket.

The fair beggars talked of returning me the alms I had given them, but I replied in such a way that they said no more about it.

"I am taken for you, sir," said the marquis, "and it may cause some annoyance to our fair friends here."

"I have foreseen that," I replied, "and I shall unmask before the end of the ball. This will falsify all suppositions, and nobody will succeed in identifying you."

"Our pockets are full of sweetmeats," said Mdlle. Q——. "Everybody wanted to fill our plates."

"Yes," said the cousin, "everybody admired us; the ladies came down from their boxes to have a closer view of us, and everyone said that no richer disguise could be imagined."

"You have enjoyed yourselves, then?"

"Yes, indeed."

"And I too. I feel quite boastful at having invented a costume which has drawn all eyes upon you, and yet has concealed your identity."

"You have made us all happy," said the lieutenant's little mistress. "I never thought I should have such a pleasant evening."

"Finis coronat opus," I replied, "and I hope the end will be even better than the beginning."

So saying I gave my sweetheart's hand a gentle pressure, and whether she understood me or not I felt her hand tremble in mine.

"We will go down now," said she.

"So will I, for I want to dance, and I am sure I shall make you laugh as
Pierrot."

"Do you know how much money you gave each of us?"

"I cannot say precisely, but I believe I gave each an equal share."

"That is so. I think it is wonderful how you could do it."

"I have done it a thousand times. When I lose a paroli of ten sequins I put three fingers into my purse, and am certain to bring up thirty sequins. I would bet I gave you each from thirty-eight to forty sequins."

"Forty exactly. It's wonderful. We shall remember this masqued ball."

"I don't think anybody will imitate us," said the marquis.

"No," said the cousin, "and we would not dare to wear the same dresses again."

We put on our masks, and I was the first to go out. After numerous little jocularities with the harlequins, especially the female ones, I recognized Therese in a domino, and walking up to her as awkwardly as I could I asked her to dance with me.

"You are the Pierrot who broke the bank?" she said.

I answered the question in the affirmative by a nod.

I danced like a madman, always on the point of falling to the ground and never actually doing so.

When the dance was over, I offered her my arm and took her back to her box, where Greppi was sitting by himself. She let me come in, and their surprise was great when I took off my mask. They had thought I was one of the beggars. I gave M. Greppi Canano's cheque, and as soon as he had handed me an acknowledgment I went down to the ball-room again with my mask off, much to the astonishment of the inquisitive, who had made sure that the marquis was I.

Towards the end of the ball I went away in a sedan-chair, which I stopped near the door of an hotel, and a little further on I took another which brought me to the door of the pastry-cook's. I found Zenobia in bed. She said she was sure I would come back by myself. I undressed as quickly as I could, and got into bed with this Venus of a woman. She was absolute perfection. I am sure that if Praxiteles had had her for a model, he would not have required several Greek beauties from which to compose his Venus. What a pity that such an exquisite figure should be the property of a sorry tailor.

I stripped her naked, and after due contemplation I made her feel how much I loved her. She was pleased with my admiration, and gave me back as much as she got. I had her entirely to myself for the first time. When we heard the trot of four horses we rose and put on our clothes in a twinkling.

When the charming beggars came in, I told them that I should be able to help in their toilette as they had not to change their chemises, and they did not make many objections.

My gaze was fixed all the while on Mdlle. Q——. I admired her charms, and I was delighted to see that she was not miserly in their display. After Zenobia had done her hair she left her to me, and went to attend on the others. She allowed me to put on her dress, and did not forbid my eyes wandering towards a large rent in her chemise, which let me see almost the whole of one of her beautiful breasts.

"What are you going to do with this chemise?"

"You will laugh at our silliness. We have determined to keep everything as a memorial of the splendid evening we have had. My brother will bring it all to the house. Are you coming to see us this evening?"

"If I were wise I should avoid you."

"And if I were wise I shouldn't ask you to come."

"That is fairly answered! Of course I will come; but before we part may I ask one kiss?"

"Say two."

Her brother and the marquis left the room, and two sedan-chairs I had summoned took off the cousins.

As soon as the marquis was alone with me he asked me very politely to let him share in the expenses.

"I guessed you were going to humiliate me."

"Such was not my intention, and I do not insist; but then you know I shall be humiliated."

"Not at all; I reckon on your good sense. It really costs me nothing. Besides, I give you my word to let you pay for all the parties of pleasure we enjoy together during the carnival. We will sup here when you like; you shall invite the company, and I will leave you to pay the bill."

"That arrangement will suit me admirably. We must be friends. I leave you with this charming attendant. I did not think that such a beauty could exist in Milan unknown to all but you."

"She is a townswoman, who knows how to keep a secret. Do you not?"

"I would rather die than tell anyone that this gentleman is the Marquis of F——."

"That's right; always keep your word, and take this trifle as a souvenir of me."

It was a pretty ring, which Zenobia received with much grace; it might be worth about fifty sequins.

When the marquis was gone, Zenobia undressed me and did my hair for the night, and as I got into bed I gave her twenty-four sequins, and told her she might go and comfort her husband.

"He won't be uneasy," said she, "he is a philosopher."

"He need be with such a pretty wife. Kiss me again, Zenobia, and then we must part."

She threw herself upon me, covering me with kisses, and calling me her happiness and her providence. Her fiery kisses produced their natural effect, and after I had given her a fresh proof of the power of her charms, she left me and I went to sleep.

It was two o'clock when I awoke ravenously hungry. I had an excellent dinner, and then I dressed to call on the charming Mdlle. Q——, whom I did not expect to find too hard on me, after what she had said. Everybody was playing cards with the exception of herself. She was standing by a window reading so attentively that she did not hear me come into the room, but when she saw me near her, she blushed, shut up the book, and put it in her pocket.

"I will not betray you," said I, "or tell anyone that I surprised you reading a prayer-book."

"No, don't; for my reputation would be gone if I were thought to be a devotee."

"Has there been any talk of the masqued ball or of the mysterious masquers?"

"People talk of nothing else, and condole with us for not having been to the ball, but no one can guess who the beggars were. It seems that an unknown carriage and four that sped like the wind took them as far as the first stage, and where they went next God alone knows! It is said that my hair was false, and I have longed to let it down and thus give them the lie. It is also said that you must know who the beggars were, as you loaded them with ducats."

"One must let people say and believe what they like and not betray ourselves."

"You are right; and after all we had a delightful evening. If you acquit yourself of all commissions in the same way, you must be a wonderful man."

"But it is only you who could give me such a commission."

"I to-day, and another to-morrow."

"I see you think I am inconstant, but believe me if I find favour in your eyes your face will ever dwell in my memory."

"I am certain you have told a thousand girls the same story, and after they have admitted you to their favour you have despised them."

"Pray do not use the word 'despise,' or I shall suppose you think me a monster. Beauty seduces me. I aspire to its possession, and it is only when it is given me from other motives than love that I despise it. How should I despise one who loved me? I should first be compelled to despise myself. You are beautiful and I worship you, but you are mistaken if you think that I should be content for you to surrender yourself to me out of mere kindness."

"Ah! I see it is my heart you want."

"Exactly."

"To make me wretched at the end of a fortnight."

"To love you till death, and to obey your slightest wishes."

"My slightest wishes?"

"Yes, for to me they would be inviolable laws."

"Would you settle in Milan?"

"Certainly, if you made that a condition of my happiness."

"What amuses me in all this is that you are deceiving me without knowing it, if indeed you really love me."

"Deceiving you without knowing it! That is something new. If I am not aware of it, I am innocent of deceit."

"I am willing to admit your innocency, but you are deceiving me none the less, for after you had ceased to love me no power of yours could bring love back again."

"That, of course, might happen, but I don't choose to entertain such unpleasant thoughts; I prefer to think of myself as loving you to all eternity. It is certain at all events that no other woman in Milan has attracted me."

"Not the pretty girl who waited on us, and whose arms you have possibly left an hour or, two ago?"

"What are you saying? She is the wife of the tailor who made your clothes. She left directly after you, and her husband would not have allowed her to come at all if he was not aware that she would be wanted to wait on the ladies whose dresses he had made."

"She is wonderfully pretty. Is it possible that you are not in love with her?"

"How could one love a woman who is at the disposal of a low, ugly fellow?
The only pleasure she gave me was by talking of you this morning."

"Of me?"

"Yes. You will excuse me if I confess to having asked her which of the ladies she waited on looked handsomest without her chemise."

"That was a libertine's question. Well, what did she say?"

"That the lady with the beautiful hair was perfect in every respect."

"I don't believe a word of it. I have learnt how to change my chemise with decency, and so as not to shew anything I might not shew a man. She only wished to flatter your impertinent curiosity. If I had a maid like that, she should soon go about her business."

"You are angry with me."

"No."

"It's no good saying no, your soul flashed forth in your denunciation. I am sorry to have spoken."

"Oh! it's of no consequence. I know men ask chambermaids questions of that kind, and they all give answers like your sweetheart, who perhaps wanted to make you curious about herself."

"But how could she hope to do that by extolling your charms above those of the other ladies? And, how could she know that I preferred you?"

"If she did not know it, I have made a mistake; but for all that, she lied to you."

"She may have invented the tale, but I do not think she lied. You are smiling again! I am delighted."

"I like to let you believe what pleases you."

"Then you will allow me to believe that you do not hate me."

"Hate you? What an ugly word! If I hated you, should I see you at all? But let's talk of something else. I want you to do me a favour. Here are two sequins; I want you to put them on an 'ambe' in the lottery. You can bring me the ticket when you call again, or still better, you can send it me, but don't tell anybody."

"You shall have the ticket without fail, but why should I not bring it?"

"Because, perhaps, you are tired of coming to see me."

"Do I look like that? If so I am very unfortunate. But what numbers will you have?"

"Three and forty; you gave them me yourself."

"How did I give them you?"

"You put your hand three times on the board, and took up forty sequins each time. I am superstitious, and you will laugh at me, I daresay, but it seems to me that you must have come to Milan to make me happy."

"Now you make me happy indeed. You say you are superstitious, but if these numbers don't win you mustn't draw the conclusion that I don't love you; that would be a dreadful fallacy."

"I am not superstitious as all that, nor so vile a logician."

"Do you believe I love you?"

"Yes."

"May I tell you so a hundred times?"

"Yes."

"And prove it in every way?"

"I must enquire into your methods before I consent to that, for it is possible that what you would call a very efficacious method might strike me as quite useless."

"I see you are going to make me sigh after you for a long time."

"As long as I can."

"And when you have no strength left?"

"I will surrender. Does that satisfy you?"

"Certainly, but I shall exert all my strength to abate yours."

"Do so; I shall like it."

"And will you help me to succeed?"

"Perhaps."

"Ah, dear marchioness; you need only speak to make a man happy. You have made me really so, and I am leaving you full of ardour."

On leaving this charming conversationalist I went to the theatre and then to the faro-table, where I saw the masquer who had won three hundred sequins the evening before. This night he was very unlucky. He had lost two thousand sequins, and in the course of the next hour his losses had doubled. Canano threw down his cards and rose, saying, "That will do." The masquer left the table. He was a Genoese named Spinola.

"The bank is prosperous," I remarked to Canano.

"Yes," he replied, "but it is not always so. Pierrot was very lucky the other night."

"You did not recognize me in the least?"

"No, I was so firmly persuaded that the beggar was you. You know who he is?"

"I haven't an idea. I never saw him before that day." In this last particular I did not lie.

"It is said that they are Venetians, and that they went to Bergamo."

"It may be so, but I know nothing about them. I left the ball before they did."

In the evening I supped with the countess, her husband, and Triulzi. They were of the same opinion as Canano. Triulzi said that I had let the cat out of the bag by giving the beggars handfuls of sequins.

"That is a mistake," I answered. "When the luck is in my favour I never refuse anyone who asks me for money, for I have a superstition that I should lose if I did. I had won thirty pounds weight of gold, and I could afford to let fools talk."

The next day I got the lottery ticket and took it to the marchioness. I felt madly in love with her because I knew she was in love with me. Neither of them were playing, and I spent two hours in their company, talking of love all the while and enjoying their conversation immensely, for they were exceedingly intelligent. I left them with the conviction that if the cousin, and not Mdlle. Q——, had been thrown in my way, I should have fallen in love with her in just the same manner.

Although the carnival is four days longer at Milan than at any other town, it was now drawing to a close. There were three more balls. I played every day, and every day I lost two or three hundred sequins. My prudence caused even more surprise than my bad fortune. I went every day to the fair cousins and made love, but I was still at the same point; I hoped, but could get nothing tangible. The fair marchioness sometimes gave me a kiss, but this was not enough for me. It is true that so far I had not dared to ask her to meet me alone. As it was I felt my love might die for want of food, and three days before the ball I asked her if she, her two friends, the marquis, and the lieutenant, would come and sup with me.

"My brother," she said, "will call on you to-morrow to see what can be arranged."

This was a good omen. The next day the lieutenant came. I had just received the drawings at the lottery, and what was my surprise and delight to see the two numbers three and forty. I said nothing to the young marquis, as his sister had forbidden me, but I foresaw that this event would be favourable to my suit.

"The Marquis of F——," said the worthy ambassador, "asks you to supper in your own rooms with all the band of beggars. He wishes to give us a surprise, and would be obliged if you would lend him the room to have a set of disguises made, and to ensure secrecy he wants you to let have the same waiting-maid."

"With pleasure; tell the marquis that all shall be according to his pleasure."

"Get the girl to come there at three o'clock to-day, and let the pastry-cook know that the marquis has full powers to do what he likes in the place."

"Everything shall be done as you suggest."

I guessed at once that the marquis wanted to have a taste of Zenobia; but this seemed to me so natural that, far from being angry, I felt disposed to do all in my power to favour his plans. Live and let live has always been my maxim, and it will be so to my dying day, though now I do but live a life of memories.

As soon as I was dressed I went out, and having told the pastrycook to consider the gentleman who was coming as myself, I called on the tailor, who was delighted at my getting his wife work. He knew by experience that she was none the worse for these little absences.

"I don't want you," said I to the tailor, "as it is only women's dresses that have to be done. My good gossip here will be sufficient."

"At three o'clock she may go, and I shall not expect to see her again for three days."

After I had dined I called as usual on the fair marchioness, and found her in a transport of delight. Her lottery ticket had got her five hundred sequins.

"And that makes you happy, does it?" said I.

"It does, not because of the gain in money, though I am by no means rich, but for the beauty of the idea and for the thought that I owe it all to you. These two things speak volumes in your favour."

"What do they say?"

"That you deserve to be loved."

"And also that you love me?"

"No, but my heart tells me as much."

"You make me happy, but does not your heart also tell you that you should prove your love?"

"Dearest, can you doubt it?"

With these words she gave me her hand to kiss for the first time.

"My first idea," she added, "was to put the whole forty sequins on the 'ambe'."

"You hadn't sufficient courage?"

"It wasn't that, I felt ashamed to do it. I was afraid that you might have a thought you would not tell me of—namely, that if I gave you the forty sequins to risk on the lottery, you would think I despised your present. This would have been wrong, and if you had encouraged me I should have risked all the money."

"I am so sorry not to have thought of it. You would have had ten thousand sequins, and I should be a happy man."

"We will say no more about it."

"Your brother tells me that we are going to the masqued ball under the direction of the marquis, and I leave you to imagine how glad I feel at the thought of spending a whole night with you. But one thought troubles me."

"What is that?"

"I am afraid it will not go off so well as before."

"Don't be afraid, the marquis is a man of much ingenuity, and loves my cousin's honour as herself. He is sure to get us disguises in which we shall not be recognized."

"I hope so. He wants to pay for everything, including the supper."

"He cannot do better than imitate your example in that respect."

On the evening of the ball I went at an early hour to the pastry-cook's, where I found the marquis well pleased with the progress that had been made. The dressing room was shut. I asked him in a suggestive manner if he was satisfied with Zenobia.

"Yes, with her work," he answered; "I did not ask her to do anything else for me."

"Oh! of course I believe it, but I am afraid your sweetheart will be rather sceptical."

"She knows that I cannot love anyone besides herself."

"Well, well, we will say no more about it."

When the guests came the marquis said that as the costumes would amuse us we had better put them on before supper.

We followed him into the next room, and he pointed out two thick bundles.

"Here, ladies, are your disguises," said he; "and here is your maid who will help you while we dress in another room."

He took the larger of the two bundles, and when we were shut up in our room he undid the string, and gave us our dresses, saying,—

"Let us be as quick as we can."

We burst out laughing to see a set of women's clothes. Nothing was wanting, chemises, embroidered shoes with high heels, superb garters, and, to relieve us of the trouble of having our hair done, exquisite caps with rich lace coming over the forehead. I was surprised to find that my shoes fitted me perfectly, but I heard afterwards that he employed the same bootmaker as I did. Corsets, petticoats, gowns, kerchief, fans, work-bags, rouge-boxes, masks, gloves-all were there. We only helped each other with our hair, but when it was done we looked intensely stupid, with the exception of the young officer, who really might have been taken for a pretty woman; he had concealed his deficiency in feminine characteristics by false breasts and a bustle.

We took off our breeches one after the other.

"Your fine garters," said I, to the marquis, "make me want to wear some too."

"Exactly," said the marquis; "but the worst of it is nobody will take the trouble to find out whether we have garters or not, for two young ladies five feet ten in height will not inspire very ardent desires."

I had guessed that the girls would be dressed like men, and I was not mistaken. They were ready before us, and when we opened the door we saw them standing with their backs to the fireplace.

They looked three young pages minus their impudence, for though they endeavoured to seem quite at their ease they were rather confused.

We advanced with the modesty of the fair sex, and imitating the air of shy reserve which the part demanded. The girls of course thought themselves obliged to mimic the airs of men, and they did not accost us like young men accustomed to behave respectfully to ladies. They were dressed as running footmen, with tight breeches, well-fitting waistcoats, open throats, garters with a silver fringe, laced waistbands, and pretty caps trimmed with silver lace, and a coat of arms emblazoned in gold. Their lace shirts were ornamented with an immense frill of Alencon point. In this dress, which displayed their beautiful shapes under a veil which was almost transparent, they would have stirred the sense of a paralytic, and we had no symptoms of that disease. However, we loved them too well to frighten them.

After the silly remarks usual on such occasions had been passed, we began to talk naturally while we were waiting for supper. The ladies said that as this was the first time they had dressed as men they were afraid of being recognized.

"Supposing somebody knew us," cried the cousin, "we should be undone!"

They were right; but our part was to reassure them, though I at any rate would have preferred to stay where we were. We sat down to supper, each next to his sweetheart, and to my surprise the lieutenant's mistress was the first to begin the fun. Thinking that she could not pretend to be a man without being impudent, she began to toy with the lady-lieutenant, who defended himself like a prudish miss. The two cousins, not to be outdone, began to caress us in a manner that was rather free. Zenobia, who was waiting on us at table could not help laughing when Mdlle. Q—- reproached her for having made my dress too tight in the neck. She stretched out her hand as if to toy with me, whereupon I gave her a slight box on the ear, and imitating the manner of a repentant cavalier she kissed my hand and begged my pardon.

The marquis said he felt cold, and his mistress asked him if he had his breeches on, and put her hand under his dress to see, but she speedily drew it back with a blush. We all burst out laughing, and she joined in, and proceeded with her part of hardy lover.

The supper was admirable; everything was choice and abundant. Warm with love and wine, we rose from the table at which we had been for two hours, but as we got up sadness disfigured the faces of the two pretty cousins. They did not dare to go to the ball in a costume that would put them at the mercy of all the libertines there. The marquis and I felt that they were right.

"We must make up our minds," said the lieutenant, "shall we go to the ball or go home?"

"Neither," said the marquis, "we will dance here."

"Where are the violins" asked his mistress, "you could not get them to-night for their weight in gold."

"Well," said I, "we will do without them. We will have some punch, laugh, and be merry, and we shall enjoy ourselves better than at the ball, and when we are tired we can go to sleep. We have three beds here."

"Two would be enough," said the cousin.

"True, but we can't have too much of a good thing."

Zenobia had gone to sup with the pastrycook's wife, but she was ready to come up again when she should be summoned.

After two hours spent in amorous trifling, the lieutenant's mistress, feeling a little dizzy, went into an adjoining room and lay down on the bed. Her lover was soon beside her.

Mdlle. Q——, who was in the same case, told me that she would like to rest, so I took her into a room where she could sleep the night, and advised her to do so.

"I don't think I need fear its going any farther," I said, "we will leave the marquis with your cousin then, and I will watch over you while you sleep."

"No, no, you shall sleep too." So saying, she went into the dressing-room, and asked me to get her cloak. I brought it to her, and when she came in she said,—

"I breathe again. Those dreadful trousers were too tight; they hurt me."
She threw herself on the bed, with nothing on besides her cloak.

"Where did the breeches hurt you?" said I.

"I can't tell you, but I should think you must find them dreadfully uncomfortable."

"But, dearest, our anatomy is different, and breeches do not trouble us at all where they hurt you."

As I spoke I held her to my breast and let myself fall gently beside her on the bed. We remained thus a quarter of an hour without speaking, our lips glued together in one long kiss. I left her a moment by herself, and when I returned she was between the sheets. She said she had undressed to be able to sleep better, and, shutting her eyes, turned away. I knew that the happy hour had come, and taking off my woman's clothes in a twinkling, I gently glided into the bed beside her, for the last struggles of modesty must be tenderly respected. I clasped her in my arms and a gentle pressure soon aroused her passions, and turning towards me she surrendered to me all her charms.

After the first sacrifice I proposed a wash, for though I could not exactly flatter myself that I had been the first to break open the lock, the victim had left some traces on the bed, which looked as if it were so. The offer was received with delight, and when the operation was over she allowed me to gaze on all her charms, which I covered with kisses. Growing bolder, she made me grant her the same privilege.

"What a difference there is," said she, "between nature and art!"

"But of course you think that art is the better?"

"No, certainly not."

"But there may be imperfections in nature, whereas art is perfect."

"I do not know whether there be any imperfection in what I behold, but I do know that I have never seen anything so beautiful."

In fact she had the instrument of love before her eyes in all its majesty, and I soon made her feel its power. She did not remain still a moment, and I have known few women so ardent and flexible in their movements.

"If we were wise," said she, "instead of going to the ball again we would come here and enjoy ourselves."

I kissed the mouth which told me so plainly that I was to be happy, and I convinced her by my transports that no man could love her as ardently as I did. I had no need to keep her awake, she shewed no inclination for sleep. We were either in action or contemplation, or engaged in amorous discourse, the whole time. I cheated her now and then, but to her own advantage, for a young woman is always more vigorous than a man, and we did not stop till the day began to break. There was no need for concealment, for each had enjoyed his sweetheart in peace and happiness, and it was only modesty which silenced our congratulations. By this silence we did not proclaim our happiness, but neither did we deny it.

When we were ready I thanked the marquis, and asked him to supper for the next ball night without any pretence of our going to the masquerade, if the ladies had no objection. The lieutenant answered for them in the affirmative, and his mistress threw her arms round his neck, reproaching him for having slept all night. The marquis confessed to the same fault, and I repeated the words like an article of faith, while the ladies kissed us, and thanked us for our kindness to them. We parted in the same way as before, except that this time the marquis remained with Zenobia.

I went to bed as soon as I got home, and slept till three o'clock. When I got up I found the house was empty, so I went to dine at the pastry-cook's, where I found Zenobia and her husband, who had come to enjoy the leavings of our supper. He told me that I had made his fortune, as the marquis had given his wife twenty-four sequins and the woman's dress he had worn. I gave her mine as well. I told my gossip that I should like some dinner, and the tailor went away in a grateful mood.

As soon as I was alone with Zenobia I asked her if she were satisfied with the marquis.

"He paid me well," she answered, a slight blush mounting on her cheeks.

"That is enough," said I, "no one can see you without loving you, or love you without desiring to possess your charms."

"The marquis did not go so far as that."

"It may be so, but I am surprised to hear it."

When I had dined, I hastened to call on the fair marchioness, whom I loved more than ever after the delicious night she had given me. I wanted to see what effect she would have on me, after making me so happy. She looked prettier than ever. She received me in a way becoming in a mistress who is glad to have acquired some rights over her lover.

"I was sure," said she, "that you would come and see me;" and though her cousin was there she kissed me so often and so ardently that there was no room for doubt as to the manner in which we had spent our night together. I passed five hours with her, which went by all too quickly, for we talked of love, and love is an inexhaustible subject. This five hours' visit on the day after our bridal shewed me that I was madly in love with my new conquest, while it must have convinced her that I was worthy of her affection.

Countess A—— B—— had sent me a note asking me to sup with her, her husband, and the Marquis Triulzi, and other friends.

This engagement prevented my paying a visit to Canano, who had won a thousand sequins of me since my great victory as Pierrot. I knew that he boasted that he was sure of me, but in my own mind I had determined to gain the mastery. At supper the countess waged war on me. I slept out at night. I was rarely visible. She tried hard to steal my secret from me, and to get some information as to my amorous adventures. It was known that I sometimes supped at Therese's with Greppi, who was laughed at because he had been silly enough to say that he had nothing to dread from my power. The better to conceal my game, I said he was quite right.

The next day Barbaro, who was as honest as most professional sharpers are, brought me the two hundred sequins I had lent him, with a profit of two hundred more. He told me that he had had a slight difference with the lieutenant, and was not going to play any more. I thanked him for having presented me to the fair marchioness, telling him that I was quite in love with her and in hopes of overcoming her scruples. He smiled, and praised my discretion, letting me understand that I did not take him in; but it was enough for me not to confess to anything.

About three o'clock I called on my sweetheart, and spent five hours with her as before. As Barbaro was not playing, the servants had been ordered to say that no one was at home. As I was the declared lover of the marchioness, her cousin treated me as an intimate friend. She begged me to stay at Milan as long as possible, not only to make her cousin happy, but for her sake as well, since without me she could not enjoy the marquis's society in private, and while her father was alive he would never dare to come openly to the house. She thought she would certainly become his wife as soon as her old father was dead, but she hoped vainly, for soon after the marquis fell into evil ways and was ruined.

Next evening we all assembled at supper, and instead of going to the ball gave ourselves up to pleasure. We spent a delicious night, but it was saddened by the reflection that the carnival was drawing to a close, and with it our mutual pleasures would be over.

On the eve of Shrove Tuesday as there was no ball I sat down to play, and not being able once to hit on three winning cards, I lost all the gold I had about me. I should have left the table as usual if a woman disguised as a man had not given me a card, and urged me by signs to play it. I risked a hundred sequins on it, giving my word for the payment. I lost, and in my endeavours to get back my money I lost a thousand sequins, which I paid the next day.

I was just going out to console myself with the company of my dear marchioness, when I saw the evil-omened masquer approaching, accompanied by a man, also in disguise, who shook me by the hand and begged me to come at ten o'clock to the "Three Kings" at such a number, if the honour of an old friend was dear to me.

"What friend is that?"

"Myself."

"What is your name?"

"I cannot tell you."

"Then you need not tell me to come, for if you were a true friend of mine you would tell me your name."

I went out and he followed me, begging me to come with him to the end of the arcades. When we got there he took off his mask, and I recognized Croce, whom my readers may remember.

I knew he was banished from Milan, and understood why he did not care to give his name in public, but I was exceedingly glad I had refused to go to his inn.

"I am surprised to see you here," said I.

"I dare say your are. I have come here in this carnival season, when one can wear a mask, to compel my relations to give me what they owe me; but they put me off from one day to another, as they are sure I shall be obliged to go when Lent begins."

"And will you do so?"

"I shall be obliged to, but as you will not come and see me, give me twenty sequins, which will enable me to leave Milan. My cousin owes me ten thousand livres, and will not pay me a tenth even. I will kill him before I go."

"I haven't a farthing, and that mask of yours has made me lose a thousand sequins, which I do not know how to pay.

"I know. I am an unlucky man, and bring bad luck to all my friends. It was I who told her to give you a card, in the hope that it would change the run against you."

"Is she a Milanese girl?"

"No, she comes from Marseilles, and is the daughter of a rich agent. I fell in love with her, seduced her, and carried her off to her unhappiness. I had plenty of money then, but, wretch that I am, I lost it all at Genoa, where I had to sell all my possessions to enable me to come here. I have been a week in Milan. Pray give me the wherewithal to escape."

I was touched with compassion, and I borrowed twenty sequins from Canano, and gave them to the poor wretch, telling him to write to me.

This alms-giving did me good; it made me forget my losses, and I spent a delightful evening with the marchioness.

The next day we supped together at my rooms, and spent the rest of the night in amorous pleasures. It was the Saturday, the last day of the carnival at Milan, and I spent the whole of the Sunday in bed, for the marchioness had exhausted me, and I knew that a long sleep would restore my strength.

Early on Monday morning Clairmont brought me a letter which had been left by a servant. It had no signature, and ran as follows:

"Have compassion, sir, on the most wretched creature breathing. M. de la Croix has gone away in despair. He has left me here in the inn, where he has paid for nothing. Good God! what will become of me? I conjure you to come and see me, be it only to give me your advice."

I did not hesitate for a moment, and it was not from any impulses of love or profligacy that I went, but from pure compassion. I put on my great coat, and in the same room in which I had seen Irene I saw a young and pretty girl, about whose face there was something peculiarly noble and attractive. I saw in her innocence and modesty oppressed and persecuted. As soon as I came in she humbly apologized for having dared to trouble me, and she asked me to tell a woman who was in the room to leave it, as she did not speak Italian.

"She has been tiring me for more than an hour. I cannot understand what she says, but I can make out that she wants to do me a service. However, I do not feel inclined to accept her assistance."

"Who told you to come and see this young lady?" said I, to the woman.

"One of the servants of the inn told me that a young lady from foreign parts had been left alone here, and that she was much to be pitied. My feelings of humanity made me come and see if I could be useful to her; but I see she is in good hands, and I am very glad of it for her sake, poor dear!"

I saw that the woman was a procuress, and I only replied with a smile of contempt.

The poor girl then told me briefly what I had already heard, and added that Croce, who called himself De St. Croix, had gone to the gaming-table as soon as he had got my twenty sequins, and that he had then taken her back to the inn, where he had spent the next day in a state of despair, as he did not dare to shew himself abroad in the daytime. In the evening he put on his mask and went out, not returning till the next morning.

"Soon after he put on his great coat and got ready to go out, telling me that if he did not return he would communicate with me by you, at the same time giving me your address, of which I have made use as you know. He has not come back, and if you have not seen him I am sure he has gone off on foot without a penny in his pocket. The landlord wants to be paid, and by selling all I have I could satisfy his claims; but, good God! what is to become of me, then?"

"Dare you return to your father?"

"Yes, sir, I dare return to him. He will forgive me when on my knees and with tears in my eyes I tell him that I am ready to bury myself in a nunnery."

"Very good! then I will take you to Marseilles myself, and in the meanwhile I will find you a lodging with some honest people. Till then, shut yourself up in your room, do not admit anyone to see you, and be sure I will have a care for you."

I summoned the landlord and paid the bill, which was a very small one, and I told him to take care of the lady till my return. The poor girl was dumb with surprise and gratitude. I said good-bye kindly and left her without even taking her hand. It was not altogether a case of the devil turning monk; I always had a respect for distress.

I had already thought of Zenobia in connection with the poor girl's lodging, and I went to see her on the spot. In her husband's presence I told her what I wanted, and asked if she could find a corner for my new friend.

"She shall have my place," cried the worthy tailor, "if she won't mind sleeping with my wife. I will hire a small room hard bye, and will sleep there as long as the young lady stays."

"That's a good idea, gossip, but your wife will lose by the exchange."

"Not much," said Zenobia; and the tailor burst out laughing.

"As for her meals," he added, "she must arrange that herself."

"That's a very simple matter," said I, "Zenobia will get them and I will pay for them."

I wrote the girl a short note, telling her of the arrangements I had made, and charged Zenobia to take her the letter. The next day I found her in the poor lodging with these worthy folks, looking pleased and ravishingly pretty. I felt that I could behave well for the present, but I sighed at the thought of the journey. I should have to put a strong restraint on myself.

I had nothing more to do at Milan, but the count had made me promise to spend a fortnight at St. Angelo. This was an estate belonging to him, fifteen miles from Milan, and the count spoke most enthusiastically of it. If I had gone away without seeing St. Angelo, he would have been exceedingly mortified. A married brother of his lived there, and the count often said that his brother was longing to know me. When we returned he would no doubt let me depart in peace.

I had made up my mind to shew my gratitude to the worthy man for his hospitality, so on the fourth day of Lent I took leave of Therese, Greppi, and the affectionate marchioness, for two weeks, and we set out on our way.

To my great delight the countess did not care to come. She much preferred staying in Milan with Triulzi, who did not let her lack for anything.

We got to St. Angelo at three o'clock, and found that we were expected to dinner.

CHAPTER XXI

An Ancient Castle—Clementine—The Fair Penitent—Lodi—A Mutual Passion

The manorial castle of the little town of St. Angelo is a vast and ancient building, dating back at least eight centuries, but devoid of regularity, and not indicating the date of its erection by the style of its architecture. The ground floor consists of innumerable small rooms, a few large and lofty apartments, and an immense hall. The walls, which are full of chinks and crannies, are of that immense thickness which proves that our ancestors built for their remote descendants, and not in our modern fashion; for we are beginning to build in the English style, that is, barely for one generation. The stone stairs had been trodden by so many feet that one had to be very careful in going up or down. The floor was all of bricks, and as it had been renewed at various epochs with bricks of divers colours it formed a kind of mosaic, not very pleasant to look upon. The windows were of a piece with the rest; they had no glass in them, and the sashes having in many instances given way they were always open; shutters were utterly unknown there. Happily the want of glass was not much felt in the genial climate of the country. The ceilings were conspicuous by their absence, but there were heavy beams, the haunts of bats, owls, and other birds, and light ornament was supplied by the numerous spiders' webs.

In this great Gothic palace—for palace it was rather than castle, for it had no towers or other attributes of feudalism, except the enormous coat-of-arms which crowned the gateway—in this palace, I say, the memorial of the ancient glories of the Counts A——B——, which they loved better than the finest modern house, there were three sets of rooms better kept than the rest. Here dwelt the masters, of whom there were three; the Count A—— B——, my friend, Count Ambrose, who always lived there, and a third, an officer in the Spanish Walloon Guards. I occupied the apartment of the last named. But I must describe the welcome I received.

Count Ambrose received me at the gate of the castle as if I had been some high and puissant prince. The door stood wide open on both sides, but I did not take too much pride to myself on this account, as they were so old that it was impossible to shut them.

The noble count who held his cap in his hand, and was decently but negligently dressed, though he was only forty years old, told me with high-born modesty that his brother had done wrong to bring me here to see their miserable place, where I should find none of those luxuries to which I had been accustomed, but he promised me a good old-fashioned Milanese welcome instead. This is a phrase of which the Milanese are very fond, but as they put it into practice it becomes them well. They are generally most worthy and hospitable people, and contrast favourably with the Piedmontese and Genoese.

The worthy Ambrose introduced me to his countess and his two sisters-in-law, one of whom was an exquisite beauty, rather deficient in manner, but this was no doubt due to the fact that they saw no polished company whatever. The other was a thoroughly ordinary woman, neither pretty nor ugly, of a type which is plentiful all the world over. The countess looked like a

Madonna; her features had something angelic about them in their dignity and openness. She came from Lodi, and had only been married two years. The three sisters were very young, very noble, and very poor. While we were at dinner Count Ambrose told me that he had married a poor woman because he thought more of goodness than riches.

"She makes me happy," he added; "and though she brought me no dower, I seem to be a richer man, for she has taught me to look on everything we don't possess as a superfluity."

"There, indeed," said I, "you have the true philosophy of an honest man."

The countess, delighted at her husband's praise and my approval, smiled lovingly at him, and took a pretty baby from the nurse's arms and offered it her alabaster breast. This is the privilege of a nursing mother; nature tells her that by doing so she does nothing against modesty. Her bosom, feeding the helpless, arouses no other feelings than those of respect. I confess, however, that the sight might have produced a tenderer sentiment in me; it was exquisitely beautiful, and I am sure that if Raphael had beheld it his Madonna would have been still more lovely.

The dinner was excellent, with the exception of the made dishes, which were detestable. Soup, beef, fresh salted pork, sausages, mortadella, milk dishes, vegetables, game, mascarpon cheese, preserved fruits—all were delicious; but the count having told his brother that I was a great gourmand, the worthy Ambrose had felt it his duty to give me some ragouts, which were as bad as can well be imagined. I had to taste them, out of politeness; but I made up my mind that I would do so no more. After dinner I took my host apart, and spewed him that with ten plain courses his table would be delicate and excellent, and that he had no need of introducing any ragouts. From that time I had a choice dinner every day.

There were six of us at table, and we all talked and laughed with the exception of the fair Clementine. This was the young countess who had already made an impression on me. She only spoke when she was obliged to do so, and her words were always accompanied with a blush; but as I had no other way of getting a sight of her beautiful eyes, I asked her a good many questions. However, she blushed so terribly that I thought I must be distressing her, and I left her in peace, hoping to become better acquainted with her.

At last I was taken to my apartment and left there. The windows were glazed and curtained as in the diningroom, but Clairmont came and told me that he could not unpack my trunks as there were no locks to anything and should not care to take the responsibility. I thought he was right, and I went to ask my friend about it.

"There's not a lock or a key," said he, "in the whole castle, except in the cellar, but everything is safe for all that. There are no robbers at St. Angelo, and if there were they would not dare to come here."

"I daresay, my dear count, but you know' it is my business to suppose robbers everywhere. My own valet might take the opportunity of robbing me, and you see I should have to keep silence if I were robbed."

"Quite so, I feel the force of your argument. Tomorrow morning a locksmith shall put locks and keys to your doors, and you will be the only person in the castle who is proof against thieves."

I might have replied in the words of Juvenal, 'Cantabit vacuus coram latrone viator', but I should have mortified him. I told Clairmont to leave my trunks alone till next day, and I went out with Count A—— B—— and his sisters-in-law to take a walk in the town.

Count Ambrose and his better-half stayed in the castle; the good mother would never leave her nursling. Clementine was eighteen, her married sister being four years older. She took my arm, and my friend offered his to Eleanore.

"We will go and see the beautiful penitent," said the count.

I asked him who the beautiful penitent was, and he answered, without troubling himself about his sisters-in-law,

"She was once a Lais of Milan, and enjoyed such a reputation for beauty that not only all the flower of Milan but people from the neighbouring towns were at her feet. Her hall-door was opened and shut a hundred times in a day, and even then she was not able to satisfy the desires aroused. At last an end came to what the old and the devout called a scandal. Count Firmian, a man of learning and wit, went to Vienna, and on his departure received orders to have her shut up in a convent. Our august Marie Therese cannot pardon mercenary beauty, and the count had no choice but to have the fair sinner imprisoned. She was told that she had done amiss, and dealt wickedly; she was obliged to make a general confession, and was condemned to a life-long penance in this convent. She was absolved by Cardinal Pozzobonelli, Archbishop of Milan, and he then confirmed her, changing the name of Therese, which she had received at the baptismal font, to Mary Magdalen, thus shewing her how she should save her soul by following the example of her new patroness, whose wantonness had hitherto been her pattern.

"Our family are the patrons of this convent, which is devoted to penitents. It is situated in an inaccessible spot, and the inmates are in the charge of a kind mother-superior, who does her best to soften the manifold austerities of their existences. They only work and pray, and see no one besides their confessor, who says mass every day. We are the only persons whom the superioress would admit, as long as some of our family are present she always let them bring whom they like."

This story touched me and brought tears to my eyes. Poor Mary Magdalen! Cruel empress! I think I have noted in another passage the source of her austere virtue.

When we were announced the mother-superior came to meet us, and took us into a large hall, where I soon made out the famous penitent amongst five or six other girls, who were penitents like herself, but I presume for trifling offences, as they were all ugly. As soon as the poor women saw us they ceased working, and stood up respectfully. In spite of the severe simplicity of her dress, Therese made a great impression on me. What beauty! What majesty brought low! With my profane eyes, instead of looking to the enormity of the offences for which she was suffering so cruelly, I saw before me a picture of innocence—a humbled Venus. Her fine eyes were fixed on the ground, but what was my surprise, when, suddenly looking at me, she exclaimed,—

"O my God! what do I see? Holy Mary, come to my aid! Begone, dreadful sinner, though thou deservest to be here more than I. Scoundrel!"

I did not feel inclined to laugh. Her unfortunate position, and the singular apostrophe she had addressed to me, pierced me to the heart. The mother-superior hastened to say,—

"Do not be offended, sir, the poor girl has become mad, and unless she really has recognized you . . . ."

"That is impossible, madam, I have never seen her before."

"Of course not, but you must forgive her, as she has lost the use of her reason."

"Maybe the Lord has made her thus in mercy."

As a matter of fact, I saw more sense than madness in this outburst, for it must have been very grievous for the poor girl to have to encounter my idle curiosity, in the place of her penitence. I was deeply moved, and in spite of myself a big tear rolled down my face. The count, who had known her, laughed, but I begged him to restrain himself.

A moment after, the poor wretch began again. She raved against me madly, and begged the mother-superior to send me away, as I had come there to damn her.

The good lady chid her with all a true mother's gentleness, and told her to leave the room, adding that all who came there only desired that she should be saved eternally. She was stern enough, however, to add, that no one had been a greater sinner than she, and the poor Magdalen went out weeping bitterly.

If it had been my fortune to enter Milan at the head of a victorious army, the first thing I should have done would be he setting free of this poor captive, and if the abbess had resisted she would have felt the weight of my whip.

When Magdalen was gone, the mother-superior told us that the poor girl had many good qualities, and if God willed that she should keep some particle of sense she did not doubt her becoming a saint like her patroness.

"She has begged me," she added, "to take down the pictures of St. Louis de Gonzaga and St. Antony from the chapel wall because she says they distract her fearfully. I have thought it my duty to yield to her request, in spite of our confessor, who says it's all nonsense."

The confessor was a rude churl. I did not exactly tell the abbess that, but I said enough for a clever woman as she was to grasp my meaning.

We left the sorrowful place in sadness and silence, cursing the sovereign who had made such ill use of her power.

If, as our holy religion maintains, there is a future life before us all, Marie Therese certainly deserves damnation, if only the oppressions she has used towards those poor women whose life is wretched enough at the best. Poor Mary Magdalen had gone mad and suffered the torments of the damned because nature had given her two of her best gifts—beauty, and an excellent heart. You will say she had abused them, but for a fault which is only a crime before God, should a fellow-creature and a greater sinner have condemned her to such a fearful doom? I defy any reasonable man to answer in the affirmative.

On our way back to the castle Clementine, who was on my arm, laughed to herself once or twice. I felt curious to know what she was laughing at, and said,—

"May I ask you, fair countess, why you laugh thus to yourself?"

"Forgive me; I was not amused at the poor girl's recognizing you, for that must have been a mistake, but I cannot help laughing when I think of your face at her wordy 'You are more deserving of imprisonment than I.'"

"Perhaps you think she was right."

"I? Not at all. But how is it that she attacked you and not my brother-in-law?"

"Probably because she thought I looked a greater sinner than he."

"That, I suppose, must have been the reason. One should never heed the talk of mad people."

"You are sarcastic, but I take it all in good part. Perhaps I am as great a sinner as I look; but beauty should be merciful to me, for it is by beauty that I am led astray."

"I wonder the empress does not shut up men as well as women."

"Perhaps she hopes to see them all at her feet when there are no more girls left to amuse them."

"That is a jest. You should rather say that she cannot forgive her own sex the lack of a virtue which she exercises so eminently, and which is so easily observed."

"I have nothing to allege against the empress's virtue, but with your leave I beg to entertain very strong doubts as to the possibility of the general exercise of that virtue which we call continence."

"No doubt everyone thinks by his own standard. A man may be praised for temperance in whom temperance is no merit. What is easy to you may be hard to me, and 'vice versa'. Both of us may be right."

This interesting conversation made me compare Clementine to the fair marchioness at Milan, but there was this difference between them: Mdlle. Q—— spoke with an air of gravity and importance, whereas Clementine expounded her system with great simplicity and an utter indifference of manner. I thought her observations so acute and her utterance so perfect and artistic, that I felt ashamed of having misjudged her at dinner. Her silence, and the blush which mounted to her face when anyone asked her a question, had made me suspect both confusion and poverty in her ideas, for timidity is often another word for stupidity; but the conversation I have just reported made me feel that I had made a great mistake. The marchioness, being older and having seen more of the world, was more skilled in argument; but Clementine had twice eluded my questions with the utmost skill, and I felt obliged to award her the palm.

When we got back to the castle we found a lady with her son and daughter, and another relation of the count's, a young abbe, whom I found most objectionable.

He was a pitiless talker, and on the pretence of having seen me at Milan he took the opportunity of flattering me in a disgusting manner. Besides, he made sheep's eyes at Clementine, and I did not like the idea of having a fellow like that for a rival. I said very dryly that I did not remember him at all; but he was not a man of delicate feeling, and this did not disconcert him in the least. He sat down beside Clementine, and taking her hand told her that she must add me to the long catalogue of her victims. She could do nothing else but laugh at silly talk of this kind; I knew it, but that laugh of hers displeased me. I would have had her say—I do not know what, but something biting and sarcastic. Not at all; the impertinent fellow whispered something in her ear, and she answered in the same way. This was more than I could bear. Some question or other was being discussed, and the abbe asked for my opinion. I do not remember what I answered, but I know that I gave him a bitter reply in the hope of putting him in a bad temper and reducing him to silence. But he was a battle charger, and used to trumpet, fife, and gun; nothing put him out. He appealed to

Clementine, and I had the mortification of hearing her opinion given, though with a blush, in his favour. The fop was satisfied, and kissed the young countess's hand with an air of fatuous happiness. This was too much; and I cursed the abbe and Clementine, too. I rose from my seat and went to the window.

The window is a great blessing to an impatient man, whom the rules of politeness in some degree constrain. He can turn his back on bores, without their being able to charge him witch direct rudeness; but people know what he means, and that soothes his feelings.

I have noted this trifling circumstance only to point out how bad temper blinds its victims. The poor abbe vexed me because he made himself agreeable to Clementine, with whom I was already in love without knowing it. I saw in him a rival, but far from endeavouring to offend me, he had done his best to please me; and I should have taken account of his good will. But under such circumstances I always gave way to ill humour, and now I am too old to begin curing myself. I don't think I need do so, for if I am ill tempered the company politely pass me over. My misfortune obliges me to submit.

Clementine had conquered me in the space of a few hours. True, I was an inflammable subject, but hitherto no beauty had committed such ravages upon me in so short a time. I did not doubt of success, and I confess that there was a certain amount of vanity in this assurance; but at the same time I was modest, for I knew that at the slightest slip the enterprise would miscarry. Thus I regarded the abbe as a wasp to be crushed as speedily as possible. I was also a victim to that most horrible of passions, jealousy; it seemed to me that if Clementine was not in love with this man-monkey, she was extremely indulgent to him; and with this idea I conceived a horrible plan of revenging my wrongs on her. Love is the god of nature, but this god is, after all, only a spoilt child. We know all his follies and frailties, but we still adore him.

My friend the count, who was surprised, I suppose, to see me contemplating the prospect for such a long time, came up to me and asked me if I wanted anything.

"I am thinking some matter over," said I, "and I must go and write one or two letters in my room till it is time for supper."

"You won't leave us surely?" said he.

"Clementine, help me to keep M. de Seingalt; you must make him postpone his letter-writing."

"But my dear brother," said the charming girl, "if M. de Seingalt has business to do, it would be rude of me to try and prevent his doing it."

Though what she said was perfectly reasonable, it stung me to the quick; when one is in an ill humour, everything is fuel for the fire. But the abbe said pleasantly that I had much better come and make a bank at faro, and as everything echoed this suggestion I had to give in.

The cards were brought in, and various coloured counters handed round, and I sat down putting thirty ducats before me. This was a very large sum for a company who only played for amusement's sake; fifteen counters were valued only at a sequin. Countess Ambrose sat at my right hand, and the abbe at my left. As if they had laid a plot to vex and annoy me, Clementine had made room for him. I took a mere accident for a studied impertinence, and told the poor man that I never dealt unless I had a lady on each side of me, and never by any chance with a priest beside me.

"Do you think it would bring you ill luck?"

"I don't like birds of ill omen."

At this he got up, and Clementine took his place.

At the end of three hours, supper was announced. Everybody had won from me except the abbe; the poor devil had lost counters to the extent of twenty sequins.

As a relation the abbe stayed to supper, but the lady and her children were asked in vain to do so.

The abbe looked wretched, which made me in a good temper, and inclined me to be pleasant. I proceeded to flirt with Clementine, and by making her reply to the numerous questions I asked, I gave her an opportunity of displaying her wit, and I could see that she was grateful. I was once more myself, and I took pity of the abbe, and spoke to him politely, asking him his opinion on some topic.

"I was not listening," said he, "but I hope you will give me my revenge after supper."

"After supper I shall be going to bed, but you shall have your revenge, and as much as you like of it, tomorrow, provided that our charming hostesses like playing. I hope the luck will be in your favour."

After supper the poor abbe went sadly away, and the count took me to my room, telling me that I could sleep securely in spite of the lack of keys for his sisters-in-law who were lodged close by were no better off.

I was astonished and delighted at the trust he put in me, and at the really magnificent hospitality (it must be remembered all things are relative) with which I had been treated in the castle.

I told Clairmont to be quick about putting my hair in curl-papers, for I was tired and in need of rest, but he was only half-way through the operation when I was agreeably surprised by the apparition of Clementine.

"Sir," said she, "as we haven't got a maid to look after your linen, I have come to beg you to let me undertake that office."

"You! my dear countess?"

"Yes, I, sir, and I hope you will make no objection. It will be a pleasure to me, and I hope to you as well. Let me have the shirt you are going to wear to-morrow, and say no more about it."

"Very good, it shall be as you please."

I helped Clairmont to carry my linen trunk into her room, and added,—

"Every day I want a shirt, a collar, a front, a pair of drawers, a pair of stocking, and two handkerchiefs; but I don't mind which you take, and leave the choice to you as the mistress, as I wish you were in deed and truth. I shall sleep a happier sleep than Jove himself. Farewell, dear Hebe!"

Her sister Eleanore was already in bed, and begged pardon for her position. I told Clairmont to go to the count directly, and inform him that I had changed my mind about the locks. Should I be afraid for my poor properties when these living treasures were confined to me so frankly? I should have been afraid of offending them.

I had an excellent bed, and I slept wonderfully. Clairmont was doing my hair when my youthful Hebe presented herself with a basket in her hands. She wished me good day and said she hoped I would be contented with her handiwork. I gazed at her delightedly, no trace of false shame appeared on her features. The blush on her cheeks was a witness of the pleasure she experienced in being useful—a pleasure which is unknown to those whose curse is their pride, the characteristic of fools and upstarts. I kissed her hand and told her that I had never seen linen so nicely done.

Just then the count came in and thanked Clementine for attending on me. I approved of that, but he accompanied his thanks with a kiss which was well received, and this I did not approve of at all. But you will say they were brother-in-law and sister-in-law? Just so, but I was jealous all the same. Nature is all-wise, and it was nature that made me jealous. When one loves and has not as yet gained possession, jealousy is inevitable; the heart must fear lest that which it longs for so be carried away by another.

The count took a note from his pocket and begged me to read it. It came from his cousin the abbe, who begged the count to apologize to me for him if he was unable to pay the twenty sequins he had lost to me in the proper time, but that he would discharge his debt in the course of the week.

"Very good! Tell him that he can pay when he likes, but warn him not to play this evening. I will not take his bets."

"But you would have no objection to his punting with ready money."

"Certainly I should, unless he pays me first, otherwise he would be punting with my money. Of course it's a mere trifle, and I hope he won't trouble himself in the least or put himself to any inconvenience to pay it."

"I am afraid he will be mortified."

"So much the better," said Clementine; "what did he play for, when he knew that he could not pay his debts if he incurred any? It will be a lesson to him."

This outburst was balm to my heart. Such is man—a mere selfish egotist, when passion moves him.

The count made no reply, but left us alone.

"My dear Clementine, tell me frankly whether the rather uncivil way in which I have treated the abbe has pained you. I am going to give you twenty sequins, do you send them to him, and to-night he can pay me honourably, and make a good figure. I promise you no one shall know about it."

"Thank you, but the honour of the abbe is not dear enough to me for me to accept your offer. The lesson will do him good. A little shame will teach him that he must mend his ways."

"You will see he won't come this evening."

"That may be, but do you think I shall care?"

"Well—yes, I did think so."

"Because we joked together, I suppose. He is a hare-brained fellow, to whom I do not give two thoughts in the year."

"I pity him, as heartily as I congratulate anyone of whom you do think."

"Maybe there is no such person"

"What! You have not yet met a man worthy of your regard?"

"Many worthy of regard, but none of love."

"Then you have never been in love?"

"Never."

"Your heart is empty?"

"You make me laugh. Is it happiness, is it unhappiness? Who can say. If it be happiness, I am glad, and if it be unhappiness, I do not care, for I do not feel it to be so."

"Nevertheless, it is a misfortune, and you will know it to have been so on the day in which you love."

"And if I become unhappy through love, shall I not pronounce my emptiness of heart to have been happiness."

"I confess you would be right, but I am sure love would make you happy."

"I do not know. To be happy one must live in perfect agreement; that is no easy matter, and I believe it to be harder still when the bond is lifelong."

"I agree, but God sent us into the world that we might run the risk"

"To a man it may be a necessity and a delight, but a girl is bound by stricter laws."

"In nature the necessity is the same though the results are different, and the laws you speak of are laid down by society."

The count came in at this point and was astonished to see us both together.

"I wish you would fall in love with one another," said he.

"You wish to see us unhappy, do you?" said she.

"What do you mean by that?" I cried.

"I should be unhappy with an inconstant lover, and you would be unhappy too, for you would feel bitter remorse for having destroyed my peace of mind."

After this she discreetly fled.

I remained still as if she had petrified me, but the count who never wearied himself with too much thinking, exclaimed,

"Clementine is rather too romantic; she will get over it, however; she is young yet."

We went to bid good day to the countess, whom we found suckling her baby.

"Do you know, my dear sister," said the count, "that the chevalier here is in love with Clementine, and she seems inclined to pay him back in his own coin?"

The countess smiled and said,—

"I hope a suitable match like that may make us relations."

There is something magical about the word "marriage."

What the countess said pleased me extremely, and I replied with a bow of the most gracious character.

We went to pay a call on the lady who had come to the castle the day before. There was a canon regular there, who after a great many polite speeches in praise of my country, which he knew only from books, asked me of what order was the cross I carried on my breast.

I replied, with a kind of boastful modesty, that it was a peculiar mark of the favour of the Holy Father, the Pope, who had freely made me a knight of the Order of St. John Lateran, and a prothonotary-apostolic.

This monk had stayed at home far from the world, or else he would not have asked me such a question. However, far from thinking he was offending me, he thought he was honouring me by giving me an opportunity of talking of my own merit.

At London, the greatest possible rudeness is to ask anyone what his religion is, and it is something the same in Germany; an Anabaptist is by no means ready to confess his creed. And in fact the best plan is never to ask any questions whatever, not even if a man has change for a louis.

Clementine was delightful at dinner. She replied wittily and gracefully to all the questions which were addressed to her. True, what she said was lost on the majority of her auditors—for wit cannot stand before stupidity—but I enjoyed her talk immensely. As she kept filling up my glass I reproached her, and this gave rise to the following little dialogue which completed my conquest.

"You have no right to complain," said she, "Hebe's duty is to keep the cup of the chief of the gods always full."

"Very good; but you know Jupiter sent her away."

"Yes, but I know why. I will take care not to stumble in the same way; and no Ganymede shall take my place for a like cause."

"You are very wise. Jupiter was wrong, and henceforth I will be Hercules.
Will that please you, fair Hebe?"

"No; because he did not marry her till after her death."

"True, again. I will be Iolas then, for . . ."

"Be quiet. Iolas was old."

"True; but so was I yesterday. You have made me young again."

"I am very glad, dear Iolas; but remember what I did when he left me."

"And what did you do? I do not remember."

"I did not believe a word he said."

"You can believe."

"I took away the gift I had made."

At these words this charming girl's face was suffered with blushes. If I had touched her with my hand, sure it would have been on fire; but the rays that darted from her eyes froze my heart.

Philosophers, be not angry if I talk of freezing rays. It is no miracle, but a very natural phenomenon, which is happening every day. A great love, which elevates a man's whole nature, is a strong flame born out of a great cold, such as I then felt for a moment; it would have killed me if it had lasted longer.

The superior manner in which Clementine had applied the story of Hebe convinced me not only that she had a profound knowledge of mythology, but also that she had a keen and far-reaching intellect. She had given me more than a glimpse of her learning; she had let me guess that I interested her, and that she thought of me.

These ideas, entering a heart which is already warm, speedily set all the senses in flames. In a moment all doubt was laid to rest; Clementine loved me, and I was sure that we should be happy.

Clementine slipped away from the table to calm herself, and thus I had time to escape from my astonishment.

"Pray where was that young lady educated?" I said to the countess.

"In the country. She was always present when my brother had his lessons, but the tutor, Sardini, never took any notice of her, and it was only she who gained anything; my brother only yawned. Clementine used to make my mother laugh, and puzzle the old tutor sadly sometimes."

"Sardini wrote and published some poems which are not bad; but nobody reads them, because they are so full of mythology."

"Quite so. Clementine possesses a manuscript with which he presented her, containing a number of mythological tales verified. Try and make her shew you her books and the verses she used to write; she won't shew them to any of us."

I was in a great state of admiration. When she returned I complimented her upon her acquirements, and said that as I was a great lover of literature myself I should be delighted if she would shew me her verses.

"I should be ashamed. I had to give over my studies two years ago, when my sister married and we came to live here, where we only see honest folks who talk about the stable, the harvest, and the weather. You are the first person I have seen who has talked to me about literature. If our old Sardini had come with us I should have gone on learning, but my sister did not care to have him here."

"But my dear Clementine," said the countess, "what do you think my husband could have done with an old man of eighty whose sole accomplishments are weighing the wind, writing verses, and talking mythology?"

"He would have been useful enough," said the husband, "if he could have managed the estate, but the honest old man will not believe in the existence of rascals. He is so learned that he is quite stupid."

"Good heavens!" cried Clementine. "Sardini stupid? It is certainly easy to deceive him, but that is because he is so noble. I love a man who is easily deceived, but they call me silly."

"Not at all, my dear sister," said the countess. "On the contrary, there is wisdom in all you say, but it is wisdom out of place in a woman; the mistress of a household does not want to know anything about literature, poetry, or philosophy, and when it comes to marrying you I am very much afraid that your taste for this kind of thing will stand in your way."

"I know it, and I am expecting to die a maid; not that it is much compliment to the men."

To know all that such a dialogue meant for me, the reader must imagine himself most passionately in love. I thought myself unfortunate. I could have given her a hundred thousand crowns, and I would have married her that moment. She told me that Sardini was at Milan, very old and ill.

"Have you been to see him?" I asked.

"I have never been to Milan."

"Is it possible? It is not far from here."

"Distance is relative, you know."

This was beautifully expressed. It told me without any false shame that she could not afford to go, and I was pleased by her frankness. But in the state of mind I was in I should have been pleased with anything she chose to do. There are moments in a man's life when the woman he loves can make anything of him.

I spoke to her in a manner that affected her so that she took me into a closet next to her room to shew me her books. There were only thirty in all, but they were chosen, although somewhat elementary. A woman like Clementine needed something more.

"Do you know, my dear Hebe, that you want more books?"

"I have often suspected it, dear Iolas, without being able to say exactly what I want."

After spending an hour in glancing over Sardini's works, I begged her to spew me her own.

"No," said she, "they are too bad."

"I expect so; but the good will outweigh the bad."

"I don't think so."

"Oh, yes! you needn't be afraid. I will forgive the bad grammar, bad style, absurd images, faulty method, and even the verses that won't scan."

"That's too much, Iolas; Hebe doesn't need so vast a pardon as all that.
Here, sir, these are my scribblings; sift the faults and the defaults. Read what you will."

I was delighted that my scheme of wounding her vanity had succeeded, and I began by reading aloud an anacreontic, adding to its beauties by the modulation of my voice, and keenly enjoying her pleasure at finding her work so fair. When I improved a line by some trifling change she noticed it, for she followed me with her eyes; but far from being humiliated, she was pleased with my corrections. The picture was still hers, she thought, though with my skilled brush I brought out the lights and darkened the shadows, and she was charmed to see that my pleasure was as great or greater than hers. The reading continued for two hours. It was a spiritual and pure, but a most intensely voluptuous, enjoyment. Happy, and thrice happy, if we had gone no farther; but love is a traitor who laughs at us when we think to play with him without falling into his nets. Shall a man touch hot coals and escape the burning?

The countess interrupted us, and begged us to join the company. Clementine hastened to put everything back, and thanked me for the happiness I had given her. The pleasure she felt shewed itself in her blushes, and when she came into the drawing-room she was asked if she had been fighting, which made her blush still more.

The faro-table was ready, but before sitting down I told Clairmont to get me four good horses for the following day. I wanted to go to Lodi and back by dinnertime.

Everybody played as before, the abbe excepted, and he, to my huge delight, did not put in an appearance at all, but his place was supplied by a canon, who punted a ducat at a time and had a pile of ducats before him. This made me increase my bank, and when the game was over, I was glad to see that everybody had won except the canon, but his losses had not spoilt his temper.

Next day I started for Lodi at day-break without telling anybody where I was going, and bought all the books I judged necessary for Clementine, who only knew Italian. I bought numerous translation, which I was surprised to find at Lodi, which hitherto had been only famous in my mind for its cheese, usually called Parmesan. This cheese is made at Lodi and not at Parma, and I did not fail to make an entry to that effect under the article "Parmesan" in my "Dictionary of Cheeses," a work which I was obliged to abandon as beyond my powers, as Rousseau was obliged to abandon his "Dictionary of Botany." This great but eccentric individual was then known under the pseudonym of Renaud, the Botanist. 'Quisque histrioniam exercet'. But Rousseau, great man though he was, was totally deficient in humour.

I conceived the idea of giving a banquet at Lodi the day after next, and a project of this kind not calling for much deliberation I went forthwith to the best hotel to make the necessary arrangements. I ordered a choice dinner for twelve, paid the earnest money, and made the host promise that everything should be of the best.

When I got back to St. Angelo, I had a sackfull of books carried into Clementine's room. She was petrified. There were more than one hundred volumes, poets, historians, geographers, philosophers, scientists—nothing was forgotten. I had also selected some good novels, translated from the Spanish, English, and French, for we have no good novels in Italian.

This admission does not prove by any means that Italian literature is surpassed by that of any other country. Italy has little to envy in other literatures, and has numerous masterpieces, which are unequalled the whole world over. Where will you find a worthy companion to the Orlando Furioso? There is none, and this great work is incapable of transalation. The finest and truest panegyric of Ariosto was written by Voltaire when he was sixty. If he had not made this apology for the rash judgement of his youthful days, he would not have enjoyed, in Italy at all events, that immortality which is so justly his due. Thirty-six years ago I told him as much, and he took me at my word. He was afraid, and he acted wisely.

If I have any readers, I ask their pardon for these digressions. They must remember that these Memoirs were written in my old age, and the old are always garrulous. The time will come to them also, and then they will understand that if the aged repeat themselves, it is because they live in a world of memories, without a present and without a future.

I will now return to my narrative, which I have kept steadily in view.

Clementine gazed from me to the books, and from the books to me. She wondered and admired, and could scarcely believe this treasure belonged to her. At last she collected herself, and said in a tone full of gratitude,—

"You have come to St. Angelo to make me happy."

Such a saying makes a man into a god. He is sure that she who speaks thus will do all in her power to make a return for the happiness which she has been given.

There is something supremely lovely in the expression of gratefulness on the face of the being one loves. If you have not experienced the feelings I describe, dear reader, I pity you, and am forced to conclude that you must have been either awkward or miserly, and therefore unworthy of love.

Clementine ate scarcely anything at dinner, and afterwards retired to her room where I soon joined her. We amused ourselves by putting the books in order, and she sent for a carpenter to make a bookcase with a lock and key.

"It will be my pleasure to read these books," said she, "when you have left us."

In the evening she was lucky with the cards, and in delightful spirits. I asked them all to dine with me at Lodi, but as the dinner was for twelve the Countess Ambrose said she would be able to find the two guests who were wanted at Lodi, and the canon said he would take the lady friend with her two children.

The next day was one of happy quiet, and I spent it without leaving the castle, being engaged in instructing my Hebe on the nature of the sphere, and in preparing her for the beauties of Wolf. I presented her with my case of mathematical instruments, which seemed to her invaluable.

I burned with passion for this charming girl; but would I have done so in her taste for literature and science had not been backed up by her personal charms? I suspect not. I like a dish pleasing to the palate, but if it is not pleasing to the eye as well, I do not taste it but put down as bad. The surface is always the first to interest, close examination comes afterwards. The man who confines himself to superficial charms, is superficial himself, but with them all love begins, except that which rises in the realm of fancy, and this nearly always falls before the reality.

When I went to bed, still thinking of Clementine, I began to reflect seriously, and I was astonished to find that during all the hours we had spent together she had not caused the slightest sensual feeling to arise in me. Nevertheless, I could not assign the reason to fear, nor to shyness which is unknown to me, nor to false shame, nor to what is called a feeling of duty. It was certainly not virtue, for I do not carry virtue so far as that. Then what was it? I did not tire myself by pursuing the question. I felt quite sure that the Platonic stage must soon come to an end, and I was sorry, but my sorrow was virtue in extremis. The fine things we read together interested us so strongly that we did not think of love, nor of the pleasure we took in each other's company; but as the saying goes, the devil lost nothing by us. When intellect enters on the field, the heart has to yield; virtue triumphs, but the battle must not last for long. Our conquests made us too sure, but this feeling of security was a Colossus whose feet were of clay; we knew that we loved but were not sure that we were beloved. But when this became manifest the Colossus must fall to the ground.

This dangerous trust made me go to her room to tell her something about our journey to Lodi, the carriages were already waiting. She was still asleep, but my step on the floor made her awake with a start. I did not even think it necessary to apologize. She told me that Tasso's Aminta had interested her to such an extent that she had read it till she fell asleep.

"The Pastor Fido will please you still more."

"Is it more beautiful?"

"Not exactly."

"Then why do you say it will please me more?"

"Because it charms the heart. It appeals to our softest feelings, and seduces us—and we love seduction."

"It is a seducer, then?"

"No, not a seducer; but seductive, like you."

"That's a good distinction. I will read it this evening. Now I am going to dress."

She put on her clothes in seeming oblivion that I was a man, but without shewing any sights that could be called indecent. Nevertheless it struck me that if she had thought I was in love with her, she would have been more reserved, for as she put on her chemise, laced her corset, fastened her garters above her knee, and drew on her boots, I saw glimpses of beauty which affected me so strongly that I was obliged to go out before she was ready to quench the flames she had kindled in my senses.

I took the countess and Clementine in my carriage, and sat on the bracket seat holding the baby on my knee. My two fair companions laughed merrily, for I held the child as if to the manner born. When we had traversed half the distance the baby demanded nourishment, and the charming mother hastened to uncover a sphere over which my eyes roved with delight, not at all to her displeasure. The child left its mother's bosom satisfied, and at the sight of the liquor which flowed so abundantly I exclaimed,—

"It must not be lost, madam; allow me to sip nectar which will elevate me to the rank of the gods. Do not be afraid of my teeth." I had some teeth in those days.

The smiling countess made no opposition, and I proceeded to carry out my design, while the ladies laughed that magic laugh which not painter can portray. The divine Homer is the only poet who has succeeded in delineating it in those lines in which he describes Andromache with the young Astyanax in her arms, when Hector is leaving her to return to the battle.

I asked Clementine if she had the courage to grant me a similar favour.

"Certainly," said she, "if I had any milk."

"You have the source of the milk; I will see to the rest."

At this the girl's face suffused with such a violent blush that I was sorry I had spoken; however, I changed the conversation, and it soon passed away. Our spirits were so high that when the time came for us to get down at the inn at Lodi, we could scarcely believe it possible, so swiftly had the time gone by.

The countess sent a message to a lady friend of hers, begging her to dine with us, and to bring her sister; while I dispatched Clairmont to a stationer's, where he bought me a beautiful morocco case with lock and key, containing paper, pens, sealing-wax, ink-well, paper knife, seal, and in fact, everything necessary for writing. It was a present I meant to give Clementine before dinner. It was delightful to watch her surprise and pleasure, and to read gratitude so legibly written in her beautiful eyes. There is not a woman in the world who cannot be overcome by being made grateful. It is the best and surest way to get on, but it must be skilfully used. The countess's friend came and brought her sister, a girl who was dazzlingly beautiful. I was greatly struck with her, but just then Venus herself could not have dethroned Clementine from her place in my affections. After the friends had kissed each other, and expressed their joy at meeting, I was introduced, and in so complimentary a manner that I felt obliged to turn it off with a jest.

The dinner was sumptuous and delicious. At dessert two self-invited guests came in, the lady's husband and the sister's lover, but they were welcome, for it was a case of the more the merrier. After the meal, in accordance with the request of the company, I made a bank at faro, and after three hours' play I was delighted to find myself a loser to the extent of forty sequins. It was these little losses at the right time which gave me the reputation of being the finest gamester in Europe.

The lady's lover was named Vigi, and I asked him if he was descended from the author of the thirteenth book of the "AEneid." He said he was, and that in honour of his ancestor he had translated the poem into Italian verse. I expressed myself curious as to his version, and he promised to bring it me in two days' time. I complimented him on belonging to such a noble and ancient family; Maffeo Vigi flourished at the beginning of the fifteenth century.

We started in the evening, and less than two hours we got home. The moon which shone brightly upon us prevented me making any attempts on Clementine, who had put up her feet in order that she might be able to hold her little nephew with more ease. The

pretty mother could not help thanking me warmly for the pleasure
I had given them; I was a universal favourite with them all.

We did not feel inclined to eat any supper, and therefore retired to
our apartments; and I accompanied Clementine, who told me that
she was ashamed at not knowing anything about the "AEneid."

"Vigi will bring his translation of the thirteenth book, and I shall
not know a word about it."

I comforted her by telling her that we would read the fine
translation by Annibale Caro that very night. It was amongst her
books, as also the version by Anguilara, Ovid's Metamorphoses,
and Marchetti's Lucreece.

"But I wanted to read the Pastor Fido."

"We are in a hurry; we must read that another time."

"I will follow your advice in all things, my dear Iolas."

"That will make me happy, dearest Hebe."

We spent the night in reading that magnificent translation in
Italian blank verse, but the reading was often interrupted by my
pupil's laughter when we came to some rather ticklish passage.
She was highly amused by the account of the chance which gave
'AEneas an opportunity of proving his love for Dido in a very
inconvenient place, and still more, when Dido, complaining of the
son of Priam's treachery, says,—

"I might still pardon you if, before abandoning me, you had left me a little Æneas to play about these halls."

Clementine had cause to be amused, for the reproach has something laughable in it; but how is it that one does not feel inclined to smile in reading the Latin—'Si quis mihi parvulus aula luderet Æneas?'. The reason must be sought for in the grave and dignified nature of the Latin tongue.

We did not finish our reading till day-break.

"What a night!" exclaimed Clementine, with a sigh.

"It has been one of great pleasure to me, has it not to you?"

"I have enjoyed it because you have."

"And if you had been reading by yourself?"

"It would have still been a pleasure, but a much smaller one. I love your intellect to distraction, Clementine, but tell me, do you think it possible to love the intellect without loving that which contains it?"

"No, for without the body the spirit would vanish away."

"I conclude from that that I am deeply in love with you, and that I cannot pass six or seven hours in your company without longing to kiss you."

"Certainly, but we resist these desires because we have duties to perform, which would rise up against us if we left them undone."

"True again, but if your disposition at all resembles mine this constraint must be very painful to you."

"Perhaps I feel it as much as you do, but it is my belief that it is only hard to withstand temptation at first. By degrees one gets accustomed to loving without running any risk and without effort. Our senses, at first so sharp set, end by becoming blunted, and when this is the case we may spend hours and days in safety, untroubled by desire."

"I have my doubts as far as I am concerned, but we shall see. Good night, fair Hebe."

"Good night, my good Iolas, may you sleep well!"

"My sleep will be haunted by visions of you."

CHAPTER XXII

*Our Excursion—Parting From Clementine—I Leave Milan With Croce's
Mistress My Arrival At Genoa*

The ancients, whose fancy was so fertile in allegory, used to figure Innocence as playing with a serpent or with a sharp arrow. These old sages had made a deep study of the human heart; and whatever discoveries modern science may have made, the old symbols may still be profitably studied by those who wish to gain a deep insight into the working of man's mind.

I went to bed, and after having dismissed Clairmont I began to reflect on my relations with Clementine, who seemed to have been made to shine in a sphere from which, in spite of her high birth, her intelligence, and her rare beauty, her want of fortune kept her apart. I smiled to myself at her doctrines, which were as much as to say that the best way of curing appetite was to place a series of appetising dishes before a hungry man, forbidding him to touch them. Nevertheless I could but approve the words which she had uttered with such an air of innocence—that if one resists desires, there is no danger of one being humiliated by giving way to them.

This humiliation would arise from a feeling of duty, and she honoured me by supposing that I had as high principles as herself. But at the same time the motive of self-esteem was also present, and I determined not to do anything which would deprive me of her confidence.

As may be imagined, I did not awake till very late the next morning, and when I rang my bell Clementine came in, looking very pleased, and holding a copy of the Pastor Fido in her hand. She wished me good day, and said she had read the first act, and that she thought it very beautiful, and told me to get up that we might read the second together before dinner.

"May I rise in your presence?"

"Why not? A man has need of very little care to observe the laws of decency."

"Then please give me that shirt."

She proceeded to unfold it, and then put it over my head, smiling all the time.

"I will do the same for you at the first opportunity," said I.

She blushed and answered, "It's not nearly so far from you to me as it is from me to you."

"Divine Hebe, that is beyond my understanding. You speak like the Cumaean sibyls, or as if you were rendering oracles at your temple in Corinth."

"Had Hebe a temple at Corinth? Sardini never said so."

"But Apollodorus says so. It was an asylum as well as a temple. But come back to the point, and pray do not elude it. What you said is opposed to all the laws of geometry. The distance from you to me ought to be precisely the same as from me to you."

"Perhaps, then, I have said a stupid thing."

"Not at all, Hebe, you have an idea which may be right or wrong, but I want to bring it out. Come, tell me."

"Well, then, the two distances differ from each other with respect to the ascent and descent, or fall, if you like. Are not all bodies inclined to obey the laws of gravitation unless they are held back by a superior force?"

"Certainly."

"And is it not the case that no bodies move in an upward direction unless they are impelled?"

"Quite true."

"Then you must confess that since I am shorter than you I should have to ascend to attain you, and ascension is always an effort; while if you wish to attain me, you have only to let yourself go, which is no effort whatever. Thus it is no risk at all for you to let me put on your shirt, but it would be a great risk for me if I allowed you to do the same service for me. I might be overwhelmed by your too rapid descent on me. Are you persuaded?"

"Persuaded is not the word, fair Hebe. I am ravished in an ecstacy of admiration. Never was paradox so finely maintained. I might cavil and contest it, but I prefer to keep silence to admire and adore."

"Thank you, dear Iolas, but I want no favour. Tell me how you could disprove my argument?"

"I should attack it on the point of height. You know you would not let me change your chemise even if I were a dwarf."

"Ah, dear Iolas! we cannot deceive each other. Would that Heaven had destined me to be married to a man like you!"

"Alas! why am I not worthy of aspiring to such a position?"

I do not know where the conversation would have landed us, but just then the countess came to tell us that dinner was waiting, adding that she was glad to see we loved one another.

"Madly," said Clementine, "but we are discreet."

"If you are discreet, you cannot love madly."

"True, countess," said I, "for the madness of love and wisdom cannot dwell together. I should rather say we are reasonable, for the mind may be grave while the heart's gay."

We dined merrily together, then we played at cards, and in the evening we finished reading the Pastor Fido. When we were discussing the beauties of this delightful work Clementine asked me if the thirteenth book of the "AEneid" was fine.

"My dear countess, it is quite worthless; and I only praised it to flatter the descendant of the author. However, the same writer made a poem on the tricks of countryfolk, which is by no means devoid of merit. But you are sleepy, and I am preventing you from undressing."

"Not at all."

She took off her clothes in a moment with the greatest coolness, and did not indulge my licentious gaze in the least. She got into bed, and I sat beside her; whereupon she sat up again, and her sister turned her back upon us. The Pastor Fido was on her night-table, and opening the book I proceeded to read the passage where Mirtillo describes the sweetness of the kiss Amaryllis had given him, attuning my voice to the sentiment of the lines. Clementine seemed as much affected as I was, and I fastened my lips on hers. What happiness! She drew in the balm of my lips with delight, and appeared to be free from alarm, so I was about to clasp her in my arms when she pushed me away with the utmost gentleness, begging me to spare her.

This was modesty at bay. I begged her pardon, and taking her hand breathed out upon it all the ecstasy of my lips.

"You are trembling," said she, in a voice that did but increase the amorous tumult of my heart.

"Yes, dearest countess, and I assure you I tremble for fear of you. Good night, I am going; and my prayer must be that I may love you less."

"Why so? To love less is to begin to hate. Do as I do, and pray that your love may grow and likewise the strength to resist it."

I went to bed ill pleased with myself. I did not know whether I had gone too far or not far enough; but what did it matter? One thing was certain, I was sorry for what I had done, and that was always a thought which pained me.

In Clementine I saw a woman worthy of the deepest love and the greatest respect, and I knew not how I could cease to love her, nor yet how I could continue loving her without the reward which every faithful lover hopes to win.

"If she loves me," I said to myself, "she cannot refuse me, but it is my part to beg and pray, and even to push her to an extremity, that she may find an excuse for her defeat. A lover's duty is to oblige the woman he loves to surrender at discretion, and love always absolves him for so doing."

According to this argument, which I coloured to suit my passions, Clementine could not refuse me unless she did not love me, and I determined to put her to the proof. I was strengthened in this resolve by the wish to free myself from the state of excitement I was in, and I was sure that if she continued obdurate I should soon get cured. But at the same time I shuddered at the thought; the idea, of my no longer loving Clementine seemed to me an impossibility and a cruelty.

After a troubled night I rose early and went to wish her good morning.
She was still asleep, but her sister Eleanore was dressing.

"My sister," said she, "read till three o'clock this morning. Now that she has so many books, she is getting quite mad over them. Let us play a trick on her; get into the bed beside her; it will be amusing to see her surprise when she wakes up."

"But do you think she will take it as a joke?"

"She won't be able to help laughing; besides, you are dressed."

The opportunity was too tempting, and taking off my dressing-gown, I gently crept into the bed, and Eleanore covered me up to my neck. She laughed, but my heart was beating rapidly. I could not give the affair the appearance of a joke, and I hoped Clementine would be some time before she awoke that I might have time to compose myself.

I had been in this position for about five minutes, when Clementine, half asleep and half awake, turned over, and stretching out her arm, gave me a hasty kiss, thinking I was her sister. She then fell asleep again in the same position. I should have stayed still long enough, for her warm breath played on my face, and gave me a foretaste of ambrosia; but Eleanore could restrain herself no longer, and, bursting into a peal of laughter, forced Clementine to open her eyes. Nevertheless, she did not discover that she held me in her arms till she saw her sister standing laughing beside the bed.

"This is a fine trick," said she, "you are two charmers indeed!"

This quiet reception gave me back my self-composure, and I was able to play my part properly.

"You see," said I, "I have had a kiss from my sweet Hebe."

"I thought I was giving it to my sister. 'Tis the kiss that Amaryllis gave to Mistillo."

"It comes to the same thing. The kiss has produced its effects, and Iolas is young again."

"Dear Eleanore, you have gone too far, for we love each other, and I was dreaming of him."

"No, no," said her sister, "Iolas is dressed. Look!"

So saying, the little wanton with a swift movement uncovered me, but at the same time she uncovered her sister, and Clementine with a little scream veiled the charms which my eyes had devoured for a moment. I had seen all, but as one sees lightning. I had seen the cornice and the frieze of the altar of love.

Eleanore then went out, and I remained gazing at the treasure I desired but did not dare to seize. At last I broke the silence.

"Dearest Hebe," said I, "you are certainly fairer than the cupbearer of the gods. I have just seen what must have been seen when Hebe was falling, and if I had been Jupiter I should have changed my mind."

"Sardini told me that Jupiter drove Hebe away, and now I ought to drive
Jupiter away out of revenge."

"Yes; but, my angel, I am Iolas, and not Jupiter. I adore you, and I seek to quench the desires which torture me."

"This is a trick between you and Eleanore."

"My dearest, it was all pure chance. I thought I should find you dressed, and I went in to wish you good day. You were asleep and your sister was dressing. I gazed at you, and Eleanore suggested that I should lie down beside you to enjoy your astonishment when you awoke. I ought to be grateful to her for a pleasure which has turned out so pleasantly. But the beauties she discovered to me surpass all the ideas I had formed on the subject. My charming Hebe will not refuse to pardon me."

"No, since all is the effect of chance. But it is curious that when one loves passionately one always feels inquisitive concerning the person of the beloved object."

"It is a very natural feeling, dearest. Love itself is a kind of curiosity, if it be lawful to put curiosity in the rank of the passions; but you have not that feeling about me?"

"No, for fear you might disappoint me, for I love you, and I want everything to speak in your favour."

"I know you might be disappointed, and consequently I must do everything in my power to preserve your good opinion."

"Then you are satisfied with me?"

"Surely. I am a good architect, and I think you are grandly built."

"Stay, Iolas, do not touch me; it is enough that you have seen me."

"Alas! it is by touching that one rectifies the mistakes of the eyes; one judges thus of smoothness and solidity. Let me kiss these two fair sources of life. I prefer them to the hundred breasts of Cybele, and I am not jealous of Athys."

"You are wrong there; Sardini told me that it was Diana of Ephesus who had the hundred breasts."

How could I help laughing to hear mythology issuing from Clementine's mouth at such a moment! Could any lover foresee such an incident?

I pressed with my hand her alabaster breast, and yet the desire of knowledge subdued love in the heart of Clementine. But far from mistaking her condition I thought it a good omen. I told her that she was perfectly right, and that I was wrong, and a feeling of literary vanity prevented her opposing my pressing with my lips a rosy bud, which stood out in relief against the alabaster sphere.

"You apply your lips in vain, my dear Iolas, the land is barren. But what are you swallowing?"

"The quintessence of a kiss."

"I think you must have swallowed something of me, since you have given me a pleasurable sensation I have never before experienced."

"Dear Hebe, you make me happy."

"I am glad to hear it, but I think the kiss on the lips is much better."

"Certainly, because the pleasure is reciprocal, and consequently greater."

"You teach by precept and example too. Cruel teacher! Enough, this pleasure is too sweet. Love must be looking at us and laughing."

"Why should we not let him enjoy a victory which would make us both happier?"

"Because such happiness is not built on a sure foundation. No, no! put your arms down. If we can kill each other with kisses, let us kiss on; but let us use no other arms."

After our lips had clung to each other cruelly but sweetly, she paused, and gazing at me with eyes full of passion she begged me to leave her alone.

The situation in which I found myself is impossible to describe. I deplored the prejudice which had constrained me, and I wept with rage. I cooled myself by making a toilette which was extremely necessary, and returned to her room.

She was writing.

"I am delighted to see you back," said she, "I am full of the poetic frenzy and propose to tell the story of the victory we have gained in verse."

"A sad victory, abhorred by love, hateful to nature."

"That will do nicely. Will each write a poem; I to celebrate the victory and you to deplore it. But you look sad."

"I am in pain; but as the masculine anatomy is unknown to you, I cannot explain matters."

Clementine did not reply, but I could see that she was affected. I suffered a dull pain in that part which prejudice had made me hold a prisoner while love and nature bade me give it perfect freedom. Sleep was the only thing which would restore the balance of my constitution.

We went down to dinner, but I could not eat. I could not attend to the reading of the translation which M. Vigi had brought with him, and I even forgot to compliment him upon it. I begged the count to hold the bank for me, and asked the company to allow me to lie down; nobody could tell what was the matter with me, though Clementine might have her suspicions.

At supper-time Clementine, accompanied by a servant, brought me a delicate cold collation, and told me that the bank had won. It was the first time it had done so, for I had always taken care to play a losing game. I made a good supper, but remained still melancholy and silent. When I had finished Clementine bade me good night, saying that she was going to write her poem.

I, too, was in the vein: I finished my poem, and made a fair copy of it before I went to bed. In the morning Clementine came to see me, and gave me her piece, which I read with pleasure; though I suspect that the delight my praises gave was equal to mine.

Then came the turn of my composition, and before long I noticed that the picture of my sufferings was making a profound impression on her. Big tears rolled down her cheeks, and from her eyes shot forth tender glances. When I had finished, I had the happiness of hearing her say that if she had known that part of physiology better, she would not have behaved so.

We took a cup of chocolate together, and I then begged her to lie down beside me in bed without undressing, and to treat me as I had treated her the day before, that she might have some experience of the martyrdom I had sung in my verses. She smiled and agreed, on the condition that I should do nothing to her.

It was a cruel condition, but it was the beginning of victory, and I had to submit. I had no reason to repent of my submission, for I enjoyed the despotism she exercised on me, and the pain she must be in that I did nothing to her, whilst I would not let her see the charms which she held in her hands. In vain I excited her to satisfy herself, to refuse her desires nothing, but she persisted in maintaining that she did not wish to go any further.

"Your enjoyment cannot be so great as mine," said I. But her subtle wit never left her without a reply.

"Then," said she, "you have no right to ask me to pity you."

The test, however, was too sharp for her. She left me in a state of great excitement, giving me a kiss which took all doubts away, and saying that in love we must be all or nothing.

We spent the day in reading, eating, and walking, and in converse grave and gay. I could not see, however, that my suit had progressed, as far as the events of the morning seemed to indicate. She wanted to reverse the medal of Aristippus, who said, in speaking of Lois, "I possess her, but she does not possess me." She wanted to be my mistress, without my being her master. I ventured to bewail my fate a little, but that did not seem to advance my cause.

Three or four days after, I asked Clementine in the presence of her sister to let me lie in bed beside her. This is the test proposed to a nun, a widow, a girl afraid of consequences, and it nearly always succeeds. I took a packet of fine English letters and explained their use to her. She took them examined them attentively, and after a burst of laughter declared them to be scandalous, disgusting, horrible in which anathema her sister joined. In vain I tried to plead their utility in defence, but Clementine maintained that there was no trusting them, and pushed her finger into one so strongly that it burst with a loud crack. I had to give way, and put my specialties in my pocket, and her final declaration was that such things made her shudder.

I wished them good night, and retired in some confusion. I pondered over Clementine's strange resistance, which could only mean that I had not inspired her with sufficient love. I resolved on overcoming her by an almost infallible method. I would procure her pleasures that were new to her without sparing expense. I could think of nothing better than to take the whole family to Milan, and to give them a sumptuous banquet at my pastry-cook's. "I will take them there," I said to myself, "without saying a word about our destination till we are on our way, for if I were to name Milan the count might feel bound to tell his Spanish countess, that she might have an opportunity of making the acquaintance of her sisters-in-law, and this would vex me to the last degree." The party would be a great treat to the sisters, who had never been in Milan, and I resolved to make the expedition as splendid as I possibly could.

When I awoke the next morning I wrote to Zenobia to buy three dresses of the finest Lyons silk for three young ladies of rank. I sent the necessary measurements, and instructions as to the trimming. The Countess Ambrose's dress was to be white satin with a rich border of Valenciennes lace. I also wrote to M. Greppi, asking him to pay for Zenobia's purchases. I told her to take the three dresses to my private lodgings, and lay them upon the bed, and give the landlord a note I enclosed. This note ordered him to provide a banquet for eight persons, without sparing expense. On the day and hour appointed, Zengbia was to be at the pastrycook's ready to wait on the three ladies. I sent the letter by Clairmont, who returned before dinner, bearing a note from Zenobia assuring me that all my wishes should be carried out. After dessert I broached my plan to the countess, telling her that I wanted to give a party like the one at Lodi, but on two conditions: the first, that no one was to know our destination till we were in the carriages, and the second, that after dinner we should return to St. Angelo.

Out of politeness the countess looked at her husband before accepting the invitation, but he cried out, without ceremony, that he was ready to go if I took the whole family.

"Very good," said I, "we will start at eight o'clock to-morrow, and nobody need be at any trouble, the carriages are ordered."

I felt obliged to include the canon, because he was a great courtier of the countess, and also because he lost money to me every day, and thus it was he, in fact, who was going to pay for the expedition. That evening he lost three hundred sequins, and was obliged to ask me to give him three day's grace to pay the money. I replied by assuring him that all I had was at his service.

When the company broke up I offered my hand to Hebe, and escorted her and her sister to their room. We had begun to read Fontenelle's "Plurality of Worlds," and I had thought we should finish it that night; but Clementine said that as she had to get up early, she would want to get to sleep early also.

"You are right, dearest Hebe, do you go to bed, and I will read to you."

She made no objection, so I took the Ariosto, and began to read the history of the Spanish princess who fell in love with Bradamante. I thought that by the time I had finished Clementine would be ardent, but I was mistaken; both she and her sister seemed pensive.

"What is the matter with you, dearest? Has Ricciardetto displeased you?"

"Not at all, he has pleased me, and in the princess's place I should have done the same; but we shall not sleep all night, and it is your fault."

"What have I done, pray?"

"Nothing, but you can make us happy, and give us a great proof of your friendship."

"Speak, then. What is it you want of me? I would do anything to please you. My life is yours. You shall sleep soundly."

"Well, then, tell us where we are going to-morrow."

"Have I not already said that I would tell you just as we are going?"

"Yes, but that won't do. We want to know now, and if you won't tell us we shan't sleep, all night, and we shall look frightful to-morrow."

"I should be so sorry, but I don't think that you could look frightful."

"You don't think we can keep a secret. It is nothing very important, is it?"

"No, it is not very important, but all the same it is a secret."

"It would be dreadful if you refused me."

"Dearest Hebe! how can I refuse you anything? I confess freely that I have been wrong in keeping you waiting so long. Here is my secret: you are to dine with me to-morrow."

"With you? Where?"

"Milan."

In their immoderate joy they got out of bed, and without caring for their state of undress, threw their arms round my neck, covered me with kisses, clasped me to their breasts, and finally sat down on my knees.

"We have never seen Milan," they cried, "and it has been the dream of our lives to see that splendid town. How often I have been put to the blush when I have been forced to confess that I have never been to Milan."

"It makes me very happy," said Hebe, "but my happiness is troubled by the idea that we shall see nothing of the town, for we shall have to return after dinner. It is cruel! Are we to go fifteen miles to Milan only to dine and come back again? At least we must see our sister-in-law."

"I have foreseen all your objections, and that was the reason I made a mystery of it, but it has been arranged. You don't like it? Speak and tell me your pleasure."

"Of course we like it, dear Iolas. The party will be charming, and perhaps, if we knew all, the very conditions are all for the best."

"It may be so, but I may not tell you any more now."

"And we will not press you."

In an ecstasy of joy she began to embrace me again, and Eleanore said that she would go to sleep so as to be more on the alert for the morrow. This was the best thing she could have done. I knew the fortunate hour was at hand, and exciting Clementine by my fiery kisses, and drawing nearer and nearer, at last I was in full possession of the temple I had so long desired to attain. Hebe's pleasure and delight kept her silent; she shared my ecstasies, and mingled her happy tears with mine.

I spent two hours in this manner, and then went to bed, impatient to renew the combat on the following day more at my ease and with greater comfort.

At eight o'clock we were all assembled round the breakfast-table, but in spite of my high spirits I could not make the rest of the company share them. All were silent and pensive; curiosity shewed itself on every face. Clementine and her sister pretended to partake the general feeling, and were silent like the rest while I looked on and enjoyed their expectancy.

Clairmont, who had fulfilled my instructions to the letter, came in and told us that the carriages were at the door. I asked my guests to follow me, and they did so in silence. I put the countess and Clementine in my carriage, the latter holding the baby on her lap, her sister and the three gentlemen being seated in the other carriage. I called out, with a laugh,

"Drive to Milan."

"Milan! Milan!" they exclaimed with one voice. "Capital! capital!"

Clairmont galloped in front of us and went off. Clementine pretended to be astonished, but her sister looked as if she had known something of our destination before. All care, however, had disappeared, and the highest spirits prevailed. We stopped at a village half-way between St. Angelo and Milan to blow the horses, and everybody got down.

"What will my wife say?" asked the count.

"Nothing, for she will not know anything about it, and if she does I am the only guilty party. You are to dine with me in a suite of rooms which I have occupied incognito since I have been at Milan; for you will understand that I could not have my wants attended to at your house, where the place is already taken."

"And how about Zenobia?"

"Zenobia was a lucky chance, and is a very nice girl, but she would not suffice for my daily fare."

"You are a lucky fellow!"

"I try to make myself comfortable."

"My dear husband," said the Countess Ambrose, "you proposed a visit to Milan two years ago, and the chevalier proposed it a few hours ago, and now we are on our way."

"Yes, sweetheart, but my idea was that we should spend a month there."

"If you want to do that," said I, "I will see to everything."

"Thank you, my dear sir; you are really a wonderful man."

"You do me too much honour, count, there is nothing wonderful about me, except that I execute easily an easy task."

"Yes; but you will confess that a thing may be difficult from the way in which we regard it, or from the position in which we find ourselves."

"You are quite right."

When we were again on our way the countess said,—

"You must confess, sir, that you are a very fortunate man."

"I do not deny it, my dear countess, but my happiness is due to the company I find myself in; if you were to expel me from yours, I should be miserable."

"You are not the kind of man to be expelled from any society."

"That is a very kindly compliment."

"Say, rather, a very true one."

"I am happy to hear you say so, but it would be both foolish and presumptuous for me to say so myself."

Thus we made merry on our way, above all at the expense of the canon, who had been begging the countess to intercede with me to give him leave to absent himself half an hour.

"I want to call on a lady," said he; "I should lose her favour forever if she came to know that I had been in Milan without paying her a visit."

"You must submit to the conditions," replied the amiable countess, "so don't count on my intercession."

We got to Milan exactly at noon, and stepped out at the pastry-cook's door. The landlady begged the countess to confide her child to her care, and shewed her a bosom which proved her fruitfulness.

This offer was made at the foot of the stairs, and the countess accepted it with charming grace and dignity. It was a delightful episode, which chance had willed should adorn the entertainment I had invented. Everybody seemed happy, but I was the happiest of all. Happiness is purely a creature of the imagination. If you wish to be happy fancy that you are so, though I confess that circumstances favourable to this state are often beyond our control. On the other hand, unfavourable circumstances are mostly the result of our own mistakes.

The countess took my arm, and we led the way into my room which I found exquisitely neat and clean. As I had expected, Zenobia was there, but I was surprised to see Croce's mistress, looking very pretty; however, I pretended not to know her. She was well dressed, and her face, free from the sadness it had borne before, was so seductive in its beauty, that I felt vexed at her appearance at that particular moment.

"Here are two pretty girls," said the countess. "Who are you, pray?"

"We are the chevalier's humble servants," said Zenobia, "and we are here only to wait on you."

Zenobia had taken it on herself to bring her lodger, who began to speak Italian, and looked at me in doubt, fearing that I was displeased at her presence. I had to reassure her by saying I was very glad she had come with Zenobia. These words were as balm to her heart; she smiled again, and became more beautiful than ever. I felt certain that she would not remain unhappy long; it was impossible to behold her without one's interest being excited in her favour. A bill signed by the Graces can never be protested; anyone with eyes and a heart honours it at sight.

My humble servants took the ladies' cloaks and followed them into the bedroom, where the three dresses were laid out on a table. I only knew the white satin and lace, for that was the only one I had designed. The countess, who walked before her sisters, was the first to notice it, and exclaimed,—

"What a lovely dress! To whom does it belong, M. de Seingalt? You ought to know."

"Certainly. It belongs to your husband who can do what he likes with it, and I hope, if he gives it you, you will take it. Take it, count; it is yours; and if you refuse I will positively kill myself."

"We love you too well to drive you to an act of despair. The idea is worthy of your nobility of heart. I take your beautiful present with one hand, and with the other I deliver it to her to whom it really belongs."

"What, dear husband! is this beautiful dress really mine? Whom am I to thank? I thank you both, and I must put it on for dinner."

The two others were not made of such rich materials, but they were more showy, and I was delighted to see Clementine's longing gaze fixed upon the one I had intended for her. Eleanore in her turn admired the dress that had been made for her. The first was in shot satin, and ornamented with lovely wreaths of flowers; the second was sky-blue satin, with a thousand flowers scattered all over it.

Zenobia took upon herself to say that the first was for Clementine.

"How do you know?"

"It is the longer, and you are taller than your sister."

"That is true. It is really mine, then?" said she, turning to me.

"If I may hope that you will deign to accept it."

"Surely, dear Iolas, and I will put it on directly."

Eleanore maintained that her dress was the prettier, and said she was dying to put it on.

"Very good, very good!" I exclaimed, in high glee, "we will leave you to dress, and here are your maids."

I went out with the two brothers and the canon, and I remarked that they looked quite confused. No doubt they were pondering the prodigality of gamesters; light come, light go. I did not interrupt their thoughts, for I loved to astonish people. I confess it was a feeling of vanity which raised me above my fellow-men-at least, in my own eyes, but that was enough for me. I should have despised anyone who told me that I was laughed at, but I daresay it was only the truth.

I was in the highest spirits, and they soon proved infectious. I embraced Count Ambrose affectionately, begging his pardon for having presumed to make the family a few small presents, and I thanked his brother for having introduced me to them. "You have all given me such a warm welcome," I added, "that I felt obliged to give you some small proof of my gratitude."

The fair countesses soon appeared, bedecked with smiles and their gay attire.

"You must have contrived to take our measures," said they; "but we cannot imagine how you did it."

"The funniest thing is," said the eldest, "that you have had my dress made so that it can be let out when necessary without destroying the shape. But what a beautiful piece of trimming! It is worth four times as much as the dress itself."

Clementine could not keep away from the looking-glass. She fancied that in the colours of her dress, rose and green, I had indicated the characteristics of the youthful Hebe. Eleanore still maintained that her dress was the prettiest of all.

I was delighted with the pleasure of my fair guests, and we sat down to table with excellent appetites. The dinner was extremely choice; but the finest dish of all was a dish of oysters, which the landlord had dressed à la maître d'hôtel. We enjoyed them immensely. We finished off three hundred of them, for the ladies relished them extremely, and the canon seemed to have an insatiable appetite; and we washed down the dishes with numerous bottles of champagne. We stayed at table for three hours, drinking, singing, and jesting, while my humble servants, whose beauty almost rivalled that of my guests, waited upon us.

Towards the end of the meal the pastry-cook's wife came in with the countess's baby on her breast. This was a dramatic stroke. The mother burst into a cry of joy, and the woman seemed quite proud of having suckled the scion of so illustrious a house for nearly four hours. It is well known that women, even more than men, are wholly under the sway of the imagination. Who can say that this woman, simple and honest like the majority of the lower classes, did not think that her own offspring would be ennobled by being suckled at the breast which had nourished a young count? Such an idea is, no doubt, foolish, but that is the very reason why it is dear to the hearts of the people.

We spent another hour in taking coffee and punch, and then the ladies went to change their clothes again. Zenobia took care that their new ones should be carefully packed in cardboard boxes and placed under the seat of my carriage.

Croce's abandoned mistress found an opportunity of telling me that she was very happy with Zenobia. She asked me when we were to go.

"You will be at Marseilles," said I, pressing her hand, "a fortnight after Easter at latest."

Zenobia had told me that the girl had an excellent heart, behaved very discreetly, and that she should be very sorry to see her go. I gave Zenobia twelve sequins for the trouble she had taken.

I was satisfied with everything and paid the worthy pastry-cook's bill. I noticed we had emptied no less than twenty bottles of champagne, though it is true that we drank very little of any other wine, as the ladies preferred it.

I loved and was beloved, my health was good, I had plenty of money, which I spent freely; in fine, I was happy. I loved to say so in defiance of those sour moralists who pretend that there is no true happiness on this earth. It is the expression on this earth which makes me laugh; as if it were possible to go anywhere else in search of happiness. 'Mors ultima linea rerum est'. Yes, death is the end of all, for after death man has no senses; but I do not say that the soul shares the fate of the body. No one should dogmatise on uncertainties, and after death everything is doubtful.

It was seven o'clock when we began our journey home, which we reached at midnight. The journey was so pleasant that it seemed to us but short. The champagne, the punch, and the pleasure, had warmed my two fair companions, and by favour of the darkness I was able to amuse myself with them, though I loved Clementine too well to carry matters very far with her sister.

When we alighted we wished each other good night, and everybody retired to his or her room, myself excepted, for I spent several happy hours with Clementine, which I can never forget.

"Do you think," said she, "that I shall be happy when you have left me all alone?"

"Dearest Hebe, both of us will be unhappy for the first few days, but then philosophy will step in and soften the bitterness of parting without lessening our love."

"Soften the bitterness! I do not think any philosophy can work such a miracle. I know that you, dear sophist, will soon console yourself with other girls. Don't think me jealous; I should abhor myself if I thought I was capable of so vile a passion, but I should despise myself if I was capable of seeking consolation in your way."

"I shall be in despair if you entertain such ideas of me."

"They are natural, however."

"Possibly. What you call 'other girls' can never expel your image from my breast. The chief of them is the wife of a tailor, and the other is a respectable young woman, whom I am going to take back to Marseilles, whence she has been decoyed by her wretched seducer.

"From henceforth to death, you and you alone will reign in my breast; and if, led astray by my senses, I ever press another in these arms, I shall soon be punished for an act of infidelity in which my mind will have no share."

"I at all events will never need to repent in that fashion. But I cannot understand how, with your love for me, and holding me in your arms, you can even contemplate the possibility of becoming unfaithful to me."

"I don't contemplate it, dearest, I merely take it as an hypothesis."

"I don't see much difference."

What reply could I make? There was reason in what Clementine said, though she was deceived, but her mistakes were due to her love. My love was so ardent as to be blind to possible—nay, certain, infidelities. The only circumstance which made me more correct in my estimate of the future than she, was that this was by no means my first love affair. But if my readers have been in the same position, as I suppose most of them have, they will understand how difficult it is to answer such arguments coming from a woman one wishes to render happy. The keenest wit has to remain silent and to take refuge in kisses.

"Would you like to take me away with you?" said she, "I am ready to follow you, and it would make me happy. If you love me, you ought to be enchanted for your own sake. Let us make each other happy, dearest."

"I could not dishonour your family."

"Do you not think me worthy of becoming your wife?"

"You are worthy of a crown, and it is I who am all unworthy of possessing such a wife. You must know that I have nothing in the world except my fortune, and that may leave me to-morrow. By myself I do not dread the reverses of fortune, but I should be wretched if, after linking your fate with mine, you were forced to undergo any privation."

"I think—I know not why—that you can never be unfortunate, and that you cannot be happy without me. Your love is not so ardent as mine; you have not so great a faith."

"My angel, if my fate is weaker than yours, that is the result of cruel experience which makes me tremble for the future. Affrighted love loses its strength but gains reason."

"Cruel reason! Must we, then, prepare to part?"

"We must indeed, dearest; it is a hard necessity, but my heart will still be thine. I shall go away your fervent adorer, and if fortune favours me in England you will see me again next year. I will buy an estate wherever you like, and it shall be yours on your wedding day, our children and literature will be our delights."

"What a happy prospect!—a golden vision indeed! I would that I might fall asleep dreaming thus, and wake not till that blessed day, or wake only to die if it is not to be. But what shall I do if you have left me with child?"

"Divine Hebe, you need not fear. I have managed that."

"Managed? I did not think of that, but I see what you mean, and I am very much obliged to you. Alas perhaps after all it would have been better if you had not taken any precautions, for surely you are not born for my misfortune, and you could never have abandoned the mother and the child."

"You are right, sweetheart, and if before two months have elapsed you find any signs of pregnancy in spite of my precautions, you have only to write to me, and whatever my fortunes may be, I will give you my hand and legitimise our offspring. You would certainly be marrying beneath your station, but you would not be the less happy for that, would you?"

"No, no! to bear your name, and to win your hand would be the crowning of all my hopes. I should never repent of giving myself wholly to you."

"You make me happy."

"All of us love you, all say that you are happy, and that you deserve your happiness. What praise is this! You cannot tell how my heart beats when I hear you lauded when you are away. When they say I love you, I answer that I adore you, and you know that I do not lie."

It was with such dialogues that we passed away the interval between our amorous transports on the last five or six nights of my stay. Her sister slept, or pretended to sleep. When I left Clementine I went to bed and did not rise till late, and then I spent the whole day with her either in private or with the family. It was a happy time. How could I, as free as the air, a perfect master of my movements, of my own free will put my happiness away from me? I cannot understand it now.

My luck had made me win all the worthy canon's money, which in turn I passed on to the family at the castle. Clementine alone would not profit by my inattentive play, but the last two days I insisted on taking her into partnership, and as the canon's bad luck still continued she profited to the extent of a hundred louis. The worthy monk lost a thousand sequins, of which seven hundred remained in the family. This was paying well for the hospitality I had received, and as it was at the expense of the monk, though a worthy one, the merit was all the greater.

The last night, which I spent entirely with the countess, was very sad; we must have died of grief if we had not taken refuge in the transports of love. Never was night better spent. Tears of grief and tears of love followed one another in rapid succession, and nine times did I offer up sacrifice on the altar of the god, who gave me fresh strength to replace that which was exhausted. The sanctuary was full of blood and tears, but the desires of the priest and victim still cried for more. We had at last to make an effort and part. Eleanore had seized the opportunity of our sleeping for a few moments, and had softly risen and left us alone. We felt grateful to her, and agreed that she must either be very insensitive or have suffered torments in listening to our voluptuous combats. I left Clementine to her ablutions, of which she stood in great need, while I went to my room to make my toilette.

When we appeared at the breakfast, table we looked as if we had been on the rack, and Clementine's eyes betrayed her feelings, but our grief was respected. I could not be gay in my usual manner, but no one asked me the reason. I promised to write to them, and come and see them again the following year. I did write to them, but I left off doing so at London, because the misfortunes I experienced there made me lose all hope of seeing them again. I never did see any of them again, but I have never forgotten Clementine.

Six years later, when I came back from Spain, I heard to my great delight that she was living happily with Count N——, whom she had married three years after my departure. She had two sons, the younger, who must now be twenty-seven, is in the Austrian army. How delighted I should be to see him! When I heard of

Clementine's happiness, it was, as I have said, on my return from Spain, and my fortunes were at a low ebb. I went to see what I could do at Leghorn, and as I went through Lombardy I passed four miles from the estate where she and her husband resided, but I had not the courage to go and see her; perhaps I was right. But I must return to the thread of my story.

I felt grateful to Eleanore for her kindness to us, and I had resolved to leave her some memorial of me. I took her apart for a moment, and drawing a fine cameo, representing the god of Silence, off my finger, I placed it on hers, and then rejoined the company, without giving her an opportunity to thank me.

The carriage was ready to take me away, and everyone was waiting to see me off, but my eyes filled with tears. I sought for Clementine in vain; she had vanished. I pretended to have forgotten something in my room, and going to my Hebe's chamber I found her in a terrible state, choking with sobs. I pressed her to my breast, and mingled my tears with hers; and then laying her gently in her bed, and snatching a last kiss from her trembling lips, I tore myself away from a place full of such sweet and agonizing memories.

I thanked and embraced everyone, the good canon amongst others, and whispering to Eleanore to see to her sister I jumped into the carriage beside the count. We remained perfectly silent, and slept nearly the whole of the way. We found the Marquis Triulzi and the countess together, and the former immediately sent for a dinner for four. I was not much astonished to find that the countess had found out about our being at Milan, and at first she seemed inclined to let us feel the weight of her anger; but the count, always fertile in expedients, told her that it was delicacy on my part not to tell her, as I was afraid she would be put out with such an incursion of visitors.

At dinner I said that I should soon be leaving for Genoa, and for my sorrow the marquis gave me a letter of introduction to the notorious Signora Isola-Bella, while the countess gave me a letter to her kinsman the Bishop of Tortona.

My arrival at Milan was well-timed; Therese was on the point of going to Palermo, and I just succeeded in seeing her before she left. I talked to her of the wish of Cesarino to go to sea, and I did all in my power to make her yield to his inclinations.

"I am leaving him at Milan," said she. "I know how he got this idea into his head, but I will never give my consent. I hope I shall find him wiser by the time I come back."

She was mistaken. My son never altered his mind, and in fifteen years my readers will hear more of him.

I settled my accounts with Greppi and took two bills of exchange on Marseilles, and one of ten thousand francs on Genoa, where I did not think I would have to spend much money. In spite of my luck at play, I was poorer by a thousand sequins when I left Milan than when I came there; but my extravagant expenditure must be taken into account.

I spent all my afternoons with the fair Marchioness sometimes alone and sometimes with her cousin, but with my mind full of grief for Clementine she no longer charmed me as she had done three weeks ago.

I had no need to make any mystery about the young lady I was going to take with me, so I sent Clairmont for her small trunk, and at eight o'clock on the morning of my departure she waited on me at the count's. I kissed the hand of the woman who had attempted my life, and thanked her for her hospitality, to which I attributed the good reception I had had at Milan. I then thanked the count, who said once more that he should never cease to be grateful to me, and thus I left Milan on the 20th of March, 1763. I never re-visited that splendid capital.

The young lady, whom out of respect for her and her family I called Crosin, was charming. There was an air of nobility and high-bred reserve about her which bore witness to her excellent upbringing. As I sat next to her, I congratulated myself on my immunity from love of her, but the reader will guess that I was mistaken. I told Clairmont that she was to be called my niece, and to be treated with the utmost respect.

I had had no opportunity of conversing with her, so the first thing I did was to test her intelligence, and though I had not the slightest intention of paying my court to her, I felt that it would be well to inspire her with friendship and confidence as far as I was concerned.

The scar which my late amours had left was still bleeding, and I was glad to think that I should be able to restore the young Marseillaise to the paternal hearth without any painful partings or vain regrets. I enjoyed in advance my meritorious action, and I was quite vain to see my self-restraint come to such a pitch that I was able to live in close intimacy with a pretty girl without any other desire than that of rescuing her from the shame into which she might have fallen if she had traveled alone. She felt my kindness to her, and said,—

"I am sure M. de la Croix would not have abandoned me if he had not met you at Milan."

"You are very charitable, but I am unable to share in your good opinion. To my mind Croce has behaved in a rascally manner, to say the least of it, for in spite of your many charms he had no right to count on me in the matter. I will not say that he openly scorned you, since he might have acted from despair; but I am sure he must have ceased to love you, or he could never have abandoned you thus."

"I am sure of the contrary. He saw that he had no means of providing for me, and he had to choose between leaving me and killing himself."

"Not at all. He ought to have sold all he had and sent you back to Marseilles. Your journey to Genoa would not have cost much, and thence you could have gone to Marseilles by sea. Croce counted on my having been interested in your pretty face, and he was right; but you must see that he exposed you to a great risk. You must not be offended if I tell you the plain truth. If your face had not inspired me with a lively interest in you, I should have only felt ordinary compassion on reading your appeal, and this would not have been enough to force me to great sacrifices of time and trouble. But I have no business to be blaming Croce. You are hurt; I see you are still in love with him."

"I confess it, and I pity him. As for myself, I only pity my cruel destiny. I shall never see him again, but I shall never love anyone else, for my mind is made up. I shall go into a convent and expiate my sins. My father will pardon me, for he is a man of an excellent heart. I have been the victim of love; my will was not my own. The seductive influence of passion ravished my reason from me, and the only thing that I blame myself for is for not having fortified my mind against it. Otherwise I cannot see that I have sinned deeply, but I confess I have done wrong."

"You would have gone with Croce from Milan if he had asked you, even on foot."

"Of course; it would have been my duty; but he would not expose me to the misery that he saw before us."

"Nay, you were miserable enough already. I am sure that if you meet him at Marseilles you will go with him again."

"Never. I begin to get back my reason. I am free once more, and the day will come when I shall thank God for having forgotten him."

Her sincerity pleased me, and as I knew too well the power of love I pitied her from my heart. For two hours she told me the history of her unfortunate amour, and as she told it well I began to take a liking for her.

We reached Tortona in the evening, and with the intention of sleeping there I told Clairmont to get us a supper to my taste. While we were eating it I was astonished at my false niece's wit, and she made a good match for me at the meal, for she had an excellent appetite, and drank as well as any girl of her age. As we were leaving the table, she made a jest which was so much to the point that I burst out laughing, and her conquest was complete. I embraced her in the joy of my heart, and finding my kiss ardently returned, I asked her without any, circumlocution if she was willing that we should content ourselves with one bed.

At this invitation her face fell, and she replied, with an air of submission which kills desire,—

"Alas! you can do what you like. If liberty is a precious thing, it is most precious of all in love."

"There is no need for this disobedience. You have inspired me with a tender passion, but if you don't share my feelings my love for you shall be stifled at its birth. There are two beds here, as you see; you can choose which one you will sleep in."

"Then I will sleep in that one, but I shall be very sorry if you are not so kind to me in the future as you have been in the past."

"Don't be afraid. You shall not find me un worthy of your esteem. Good night; we shall be good friends."

Early the next morning I sent the countess's letter to the bishop, and an hour afterwards, as I was at breakfast, an old priest came to ask me and the lady with me to dine with my lord. The countess's letter did not say anything about a lady, but the prelate, who was a true Spaniard and very polite, felt that as I could not leave my real or false niece alone in the inn I should not have accepted the invitation if she had not been asked as well. Probably my lord had heard of the lady through his footmen, who in Italy are a sort of spies, who entertain their masters with the scandalous gossip of the place. A bishop wants something more than his breviary to amuse him now that the apostolic virtues have grown old-fashioned and out of date; in short, I accepted the invitation, charging the priest to present my respects to his lordship.

My niece was delightful, and treated me as if I had no right to feel any resentment for her having preferred her own bed to mine. I was pleased with her behaviour, for now that my head was cool I felt that she would have degraded herself if she had acted otherwise. My vanity was not even wounded, which is so often the case under similar circumstances. Self-love and prejudice prevent a woman yielding till she has been assiduously courted, whereas I had asked her to share my bed in an off-hand manner, as if it were a mere matter of form. However, I should not have done it unless it had been for the fumes of the champagne and the Somard, with which we had washed down the delicious supper mine host had supplied us with. She had been flattered by the bishop's invitation, but she did not know whether I had accepted for her as well as myself; and when I told her that we were going out to dinner together, she was wild with joy. She made a careful toilette, looking very well for a traveller, and at noon my lord's carriage came to fetch us.

211

The prelate was a tall man, two inches taller than myself; and in spite of the weight of his eighty years, he looked well and seemed quite active, though grave as became a Spanish grandee. He received us with a politeness which was almost French, and when my niece would have kissed his hand, according to custom, he affectionately drew it back, and gave her a magnificent cross of amethysts and brilliants to kiss. She kissed it with devotion, saying,—

"This is what I love."

She looked at me as she said it, and the jest (which referred to her lover La Croix or Croce) surprised me.

We sat down to dinner, and I found the bishop to be a pleasant and a learned man. We were nine in all; four priests, and two young gentlemen of the town, who behaved to my niece with great politeness, which she received with all the manner of good society. I noticed that the bishop, though he often spoke to her, never once looked at her face. My lord knew what danger lurked in those bright eyes, and like a prudent greybeard he took care not to fall into the snare. After coffee had been served, we took leave, and in four hours we left Tortona, intending to lie at Novi.

In the course of the afternoon my fair niece amused me with the wit and wisdom of her conversation. While we were supping I led the conversation up to the bishop, and then to religion, that I might see what her principles were. Finding her to be a good Christian, I asked her how she could allow herself to make a jest when she kissed the prelate's cross.

"It was a mere chance," she said. "The equivocation was innocent because it was not premeditated, for if I had thought it over I should never have said such a thing."

I pretended to believe her; she might possibly be sincere. She was extremely clever, and my love for her was becoming more and more ardent, but my vanity kept my passion in check. When she went to bed I did not kiss her, but as her bed had no screen as at Tortona, she waited until she thought I was asleep to undress herself. We got to Genoa by noon the next day.

Pogomas had got me some rooms and had forwarded me the address. I visited it, and found the apartment to consist of four well-furnished rooms, thoroughly comfortable, as the English, who understand how to take their ease, call it. I ordered a good dinner, and sent to tell Pogomas of my arrival.

The End

www.ingramcontent.com/pod-product-compliance
Lightning Source LLC
Chambersburg PA
CBHW070004300526
45794CB00001B/180